INDEX ON CENSORSHIP 4 1999

WEBSITE NEWS UPDATED EVERY TWO WEEKS

www.indexoncensorship.org
contact@indexoncensorship.org
tel: 0171-278 2313
fax: 0171-278 1878

Volume 28 No 4 July/August 1999 Issue 189

Index on Censorship (ISSN 0306-4220) is published bi-monthly by a non-profit-making company: Writers & Scholars International Ltd, Lancaster House, 33 Islington High Street, London N1 9LH. *Index on Censorship* is associated with Writers & Scholars Educational Trust, registered charity number 325003
Periodicals postage: (US subscribers only) paid at Newark, New Jersey.
Postmaster: send US address changes to *Index on Censorship* c/o Mercury Airfreight International Ltd Inc, 365 Blair Road, Avenel, NJ 07001, USA
© This selection Writers & Scholars International Ltd, London 1999
© Contributors to this issue, except where otherwise indicated

Subscriptions (6 issues per annum)
Individuals: UK £39, US $52, rest of world £45
Institutions: UK £44, US $80, rest of world £50
Speak to Tony Callaghan on 0171 278 2313

Index on Censorship and Writers and Scholars
Educational Trust would like to thank
The Arts Council of England
and
The John S. Cohen Foundation
for their support for this issue on tribes

Funded by
THE
ARTS
COUNCIL
OF ENGLAND

EDITORIAL

Poisoned land

We go to press in the second precarious week of peace in Kosovo, a place now haunted by the savageries of ethnic cleansing, where a superhuman effort of will and humanity will be needed for Albanians and Serbs to live together again. In Ivo Zanic's words, the modern history of the Balkans demonstrates all too painfully that 'the mentality that fostered the myth of Greater Serbia is by no means exclusive to the Serbs' (p157).

But ethnic cleansing, 'the special curse of the twentieth century', has a long history. *Index*, which for over a quarter of a century has monitored censorship and silencing in so many countries, reports for the first time on the original ethnic cleansing: the wars against tribal peoples that have decimated whole populations and led to the loss of at least 5,000 languages in the last 100 years alone.

But relocating populations, eradicating people and cultures has not been enough for colonialists. The assault on tribal languages reflects, as Hugh Brody says, 'a compulsion to achieve a final and decisive silence', to put an end even to the voices of the fragmented and marginalised survivors. Why was this necessary? The answer lies in the claim that tribal peoples make to the places that are theirs. So this issue of *Index* is about the battles, still going on, for land as well as language.

Meanwhile, is the land in Kosovo contaminated with depleted uranium (DU)? The British government's draft legislation on Freedom of Information (p19) would ensure you'd never get an answer to this question. But as far back as 7 May, the US Defence Department admitted that A–10 aircraft were firing DU ammunition in Kosovo. DU is both toxic and radioactive, but NATO insists that it is no more dangerous than any other heavy metal. Published material suggests this may be misleading: there are extensive reports from southern Iraq of stillbirths, birth defects and leukaemia in children born since 1991, when DU was used in the Gulf War. According to the Coghill Research Laboratories, one particle of DU material in the lungs is equivalent to a chest X-ray per hour for life. Already in Macedonia, ecologists report evidence of increased radioactivity, while the local media claim that the people of Skopje have begun to restrict their movements outdoors. ❏

contents

'Mending the broken strings' –
resurrection in the Kalahari

p76

China's punk revolution rocks
the harmonious society

p185

Plus: UK government favours secrecy over the
right to know   p19

LETTERS

Response to Dennis Nilsen
From Carl Stotton, Brighton

I read with great interest your letter to the *Daily Express*, concerning Dennis Nilsen's letter to yourselves.

Of course this subject will raise a great debate. Nilsen claims that being locked up is punishment enough for his crimes whilst claiming that he has human rights as the rest of society does. With all due respect, Nilsen gave up these rights when he murdered and butchered away the rights of so many others. Nilsen hardly makes for a good spokesperson concerning the issue of censorship within the prison system. He committed the most dreadful of crimes. This has dehumanised him, which raises the issue of freedom of expression.

Nilsen has been put away to protect society. Are we, as a society, prepared to put up with Nilsen's whims and complaints against the prison service? Is it not enough that he is being kept at the tax-payers' expense, taxes that I pay, my family pays, the victims' families pay? Please do let me assure you that life for the victim outside is far worse than the life that Nilsen will endure inside. He is so arrogant to expect that he be shown respect as a human being, though he cares nothing for the plight of his victims either living or dead. How can we allow such a man the right to freedom of speech?

In my opinion Nilsen has no rights at all. He once had the freedom of choice as we all do. He chose to go against society and humanity and now he must pay the price for his selfish action: there is after all nothing more selfish than the act of murder.

By publishing his letter, you have allowed Nilsen the freedom to speak. He did not use this opportunity for anyone else's gain other than his own, but this is typical of Nilsen. We must all bear in mind that Nilsen is in prison to be punished, not to be catered to or pampered.

The indispensability of truth
From Theo Theocharis

Science is the endeavour to discover the non-obvious truths – of both nature and society. In the thick smoke of the suffocating information overload, free expression ensures that unpopular truths may be communicated, debated, and better evaluated.

Truth must be unique, objective, unchangeable, invariable, theory-free, ideology-transcendent, universal, eternal, ultimate, absolute; and also in principle (but perhaps difficult in practice) discoverable, accessible, attainable, knowable, comprehensible, verifiable, effable, and communicable. Any use of the term 'truth' which does not satisfy one or more of the above defining features is fatally flawed, and is bound to lead, sooner or later, to 'anything goes', as indeed it has. The post-modernist and 'politically correct' idea of 'truth': subjective, relative, parochial, ephemeral, transient, theory-laden, ideology-dependent, falsifiable, unprovable, changeable, variable, surreal; as well as the traditional religious idea of 'truth': untestable, unknowable, incomprehensible, ineffable, transcendental, other-worldly; (or a confused mixture of the two – eg, Popperism) are of course meaningless, incoherent, untenable and untrue.

Proven truths entail rational certaintism and dogmatism. Thus the valid proposition 'healthy degree of scepticism' must be complemented by the equally valid, and equally indispensable, proposition 'healthy degree of dogmatism'.

The post-modernist revolution succeeded in replacing the concept of permanent truth with the transient paradigm of (transient)

paradigm; 'healthy dogmatism' with unhealthy (and invariably bogus) humilitism; not only in the social sciences but also in the physical sciences.

Any 'paradigm' that appears merely to work and does not claim to be (at least an approximation to) a truth of nature is a Santa Claus-type infantile theory and cannot legitimately claim to be scientific. For sound scientific practice in general, the words 'truth' and 'reality' are indispensable.

Moreover, any non-accidental advancement (both theoretical and practical) in every scientific field is heavily predicated on knowing and using correctly a theory that is close to the truth. In fact the closer the practised theory is to the truth, the greater the probability of advancement. In genuine science, the 'but-the-theory-works' theory of knowledge does not really work.

Significantly, the keynote article 'The uses and abuses of science' by Colin Tudge in the 'Big Science & little white lies' issue of *Index on Censorship* (3/1999) recommends humility and generally promotes a post-modern version of science, whereas any hint that these ideas have ever been criticised is completely absent.

Libraries and intellectual freedom

From Carsten Frederiksen, FAIFE, Copenhagen. E-mail faife@ifla.org

Issue 2/1999 of *Index on Censorship* was dedicated to the power of words, or more specifically to libraries. Being a librarian I can only welcome such attention. Unfortunately there was no mention of the recent and significant initiative concerning libraries and intellectual freedom.

In September 1997 IFLA, the International Federation of Library Associations and Institutions launched a special committee on Free Access to Information and Freedom of Expression (FAIFE). The Committee consists of members from 27 associations worldwide.

FAIFE monitors the state of intellectual freedom within the library community and responds to violations of free access to information and freedom of expression. The aim is to highlight the democratic mission of libraries.

Libraries are arsenals of liberty. But they can also be victims of censorship or limited access. A report from Zambia tells of uneven distribution, restrictive regulations and lack of awareness of the right of access. In Ekaterinburg books by modern philosophers have been publicly burned by order of the Russian Orthodox Church. In Orange, Toulon, Marignane and Vitrolles the *Front National* have sacked library staff and excluded certain books and newspapers.

Article 19 expresses rights which are at the very heart of librarianship, a framework needed more than ever in a world shaped by new technology and globalisation. The issue of *Index*, focusing on the book and literature, in fact reflected a somewhat outdated image of libraries. Modern libraries are active agents in the information society and defined by the increasing use of electronic resources. Some major concerns over intellectual freedom derive from this, such as legislative attempts to restrict access to information, software designed to filter Internet content and the trend towards tightening intellectual property rights.

An international framework to deal with these issues is taking form. It will be a long and hard path to travel. But the creation of FAIFE brings the principles of human rights to the core of both IFLA politics and praxis. ❏

● **Never mind the bollocks** In what has been hailed as 'a victory of sense over censorship', London Underground ruled in June that the word 'bollocks' is not a 'four-letter word' and therefore can be openly viewed by its passengers. Among the latest additions to the 'Poems on the Underground' series is an 11-line poem, *Quark*, by Jo Shapcott that includes the offending word. Along with a dozen others, it will be posted in Tube carriages and sent to 1,500 schools as representative of poetry in English over the millennium.

● **... it's the Shag Doctors** The pint-sized scourge of the sprawling *Star Wars* empire, *The Spy Who Shagged Me*, is having a hard time living up to its title. In May, Singapore's board of film censors demanded it be changed to *The Spy Who Shioked Me*. Apparently the word means 'good' or 'nice' in 'Singlish', the enclave's eclectic cocktail of English, Malay and Chinese. Back home, where 'bollocks' is fancy-free and out on the town, 'shag' is still in stir. The Odeon and ABC cinema chains have censored the title altogether, advertising it at their UK cinemas only as *Austin Powers 2*.

● **What and with what and to whom** Prostitutes who advertise via 'tart cards' blue-tacked inside Britain's phone boxes are to face fines of up to £1,000 (US$1,600) under a plan unveiled on 18 May. British Telecom (BT), which recently unveiled record profits of over £3 billion (US$4.8bn) – to considerable public fury – claims to remove 150,000 tart cards a week, or 13 million a year. Leave aside the impact on profits of a slump in clients' calls, not to mention a ban on what has become a stylish 'collectable'; it seems BT's heart-warming advertising slogan – 'It's good to talk' – rather depends on what you want to talk about – and to whom.

● **Dumb creatures** UK publisher Macmillan is standing four-square against demands by animal rights activists to revise aspects of the *Just William* stories, written by Richmal Crompton in the 1930s. The Royal Society for the Prevention of Cruelty to Animals and the National Canine Defence League complain that William's prelapsarian gang, the Outlaws, set a squalid example to today's children with their passion for collecting birds' eggs and setting dogs' tails on fire. Macmillan will defend every word the saintly Crompton wrote. What's this? An out-of-print manuscript, *William and the Nasties*, in which the short-trousered hero remodels the Outlaws on the lines of a contemporary German political movement and then sets about making life insufferable for the local, hook-nosed grocer.

● **Decree nisi** After 800 years of established practice, British civil courts issued a death sentence on Latin legal terminology in April in a bid to catch up with plain English. Out go 'writ', '*ex parte* hearing', 'guardian *ad litem*' and '*in camera*'. In their stead, Cool Britannia is to welcome 'claim form', 'hearing without notice to the other side', 'litigation friend' and 'in private'. And wigs? 'Oh, we wouldn't touch the wig,' said a source in the Lord Chancellor's office. 'You can only take reform so far, you know.'

● **Nuts** US District Judge Dee Benson refused to allow Salt Lake City high school sophomore John Ouimette to attend school wearing a T-shirt reading 'Vegan'. Benson said that veganism was inseparable from the Straight Edge movement, which police consider a violent gang. Ouimette, who denies he is a Straight Edger, was back one month later with a new T-shirt reading 'Vegans have First Amendment Rights'.

● **The fourth 'R'** Under a law that sailed through the state's two legislatures in June, Louisiana schoolchildren must address their teachers and other school staff as 'Sir' or 'Ma'am' The aim is to add 'respect' to the other three 'Rs'. 'I think it will make students better behaved,' said

Democratic representative Charles Hudson. Hudson's home town recently passed a 'baggy pants ordinance' forbidding trousers slung so low they reveal the garments beneath.

● **Going, going, Gong** With the 10th anniversary of the Tiananmen Square massacre safely behind them, China's leaders are limbering up for action against what may be the last, large-scale, organised threat to Communist rule – practitioners of the Falun Gong school of yoga-like exercises. Falun Gong was outlawed in January when President Jiang Zemin declared a 'war on cults'. This triggered a day-long silent vigil outside the 'leadership compound' on 25 April by thousands of members. On 14 June, Beijing banned the group from holding further meetings.

● **Get it straight** Two months after the capture of Kurdish leader Abdallah Oçalan, Turkey's interior ministry faxed Turkish Radio-TV Company (TRT) and the Anatolian News Agency (AA) a new language for reporting the 15-year insurrection. Thirty-seven 'hazardous' words are listed, with their approved alternatives. 'Guerrilla' and 'rebel' must bow to 'terrorist, brigand or highwayman'. Instead of *Peshmergas*, Kurdish 'highwaymen' in Iraq are denominated 'Northern Iraqis'. 'Oçalan the Terrorist' replaces Oçalan's nickname, 'Apo', familiar alike to newspaper readers – and children who refuse to go to bed on time ('Apo will get you!').

● **Safety procedures** A £13 million (US$20.8m) survey of 300 airports whose computers might fail because of the Y2K bug will remain under wraps until after the millenium. The International Air Transport Association says it would be 'scaremongering' to publicise destinations that are potentially unsafe.

● **Knee in mouth** Donald Findlay QC, bewhiskered vice-chair of Glasgow Rangers, was forced to resign in June after singing anti-Catholic songs at a barney to celebrate winning the Scottish Cup. One of the songs, 'The Billy Boys', includes a reference to being 'knee-deep in Fenian blood'. Chairman David Murray said Findlay had paid the price for a serious error of judgement. 'We cannot, on the one hand, say

we have a policy of trying to improve the sectarian issue, and then
approve an evening such as this.'

● **Native unrest** On 13 April five demonstrators filed a lawsuit
against Cleveland for wrongful arrest, illegal imprisonment and violation
of the right to free speech. The five, who included president of the
National Coalition on Racism in Sports and Media, Vernon Bellecourt,
were arrested three days earlier for burning an effigy of the mascot of the
Cleveland Indians baseball side, Chief Wahoo. Bellecourt, meantime, was
getting prickly about the exploitation of Indian names by the military.
An army regulation decrees that US aircraft be named after American
Indian tribes to accent their 'mobility, firepower and endurance' – hence
Apache, Black Hawk and Chinook. 'Black Hawk was a great leader and
a man of peace,' said Bellecourt. '[This] creates the impression that all we
did was go around fighting.'

● **Marriage guidance** Egypt's People's Assembly has finally struck
down its infamous Article 291. This exempts a rapist from punishment if
he marries his victim; the loophole has been used for centuries to avoid
prosecution. In May, the Islamic Research Academy of Al Azhar,
supreme religious authority in the land, called for the criminalisation of
urfi, a temporary sexual marriage contract used by the rich to keep
mistresses without losing their respectability. Across the Red Sea, Saudi
Grand Mufti Nasr Farid Wassel has hinted at the possibility that women
will be allowed to officiate at marriage ceremonies. Next? Girl bands?

● **Prayer crime** The Catholic Archbishop of Trinidad and Tobago
was banned from holding a vigil against the death penalty in Wildflower
Park on 6 June, on the grounds that 'prayer' was forbidden by law in any
part of the botanic gardens. The park has always been used for religious
gatherings, notably Catholic Charismatic revivals. The ministry of
agriculture, which issued the ban, was alarmed by Archbishop Pantin's
opposition to the nine hangings planned to start on 11 June. The
government repeatedly claims that its determination to apply the death
penalty is driven by public desire for the extreme punishment as a
deterrent to crime. The Catholic Church is the only religious group to
oppose capital punishment in the islands.

● **Delta of anger** On 29 May, as Nigeria's new civilian administration was being sworn in, armed Ijaw youths near the oil town of Warri sacked four of their neighbour's villages. The Itsekiris counter attacked. A traditional ruler was beheaded; 200 people lost their lives.

Violence erupts with sudden intensity in the Delta, an area that promises something far larger than the Ogoni tragedy four years ago when writer Ken Saro-Wiwa and eight others were hanged by the Abacha regime. There is the faint echo of a Rwanda in the making: communities seek to redress old wrongs; the word 'genocide' is bounced around.

Few in the Delta believe that democracy will change their lives. The military could have solved the area's problems, but chose to contain the Delta by force. The filibustering that accompanies representative rule will ensure that the region continues to boil – and to threaten the entire democratic experiment.

Across nine of Nigeria's 36 states, Delta youths now spearhead demands not just for equity from the state, but in the redistribution of income from their oil. The movement has not always been so vigorous. A first attempt at secession was led by Isaac Adaka Boro, who called for a Niger Delta Republic in 1965. The revolution was so short-lived that it earned barely a footnote in Nigerian history, but in 1990 a new phase began with the Movement for the Survival of the Ogoni People. It threatened the dictatorship and the western oil companies so severely that the whole of Ogoniland was militarised.

The killing of the Ogoni was supposed to deter other restive Delta peoples; instead it pointed the way. On 11 December 1998, 5,000 Ijaws signed a declaration in Kaiama – Adaka Boro's birthplace – that asserted their ownership of all the resources in their swamps and creeks, and gave notice to oil companies in the area. A Niger Delta Volunteer Force, patterned after Boro's army, claims to have 6,500 members and has promised to go to war.

The Ijaws have a greater capacity for resistance than the Ogonis. Though they lack a leader with the standing of Saro-Wiwa, they are spread over seven states and, at 12 million strong, are the fourth largest tribe in Nigeria. Other Delta groups have taken their cue and are canvassing for a united minorities front.

Some attempt has been made to address the crisis since Kaiama. The last military regime promised to up the revenue from central government to resource-producing states from 3 to 13 percent; it also promised N15.3 million (cUS$184,000) in development funding. Despite further pledges from the new state and federal governments, the violence continues.

There is no shortage of remedies, but politicians have always danced around the real Delta issue. A federation on paper, Nigeria has been run as a unitary state with the regions as appendages of the centre rather than equal partners. Activists in and out of the Delta have clamoured for a Sovereign National Conference to

address the question of nationalities and minorities, as well as the relation between the centre and the federal units. Until that issue is resolved, the Delta will continue to bubble and burn.
Waziri Adio

● **On message** The seriousness with which regional elites regard *Al-Jazeera* Satellite Channel (JSC) was underlined in June when Israel stripped Palestinian prisoners of the right to watch it for 'fear of incitement'.

In its three years of rare pluralistic broadcasting, Qatar-based JSC has been toasted as 'the darling of Arab viewers' (*Financial Times*), 'la petite CNN du Golfe' (*Libération*) and 'the biggest phenomenon in regional broadcasting' (*Middle East Insight*). Established in February 1996 and employing staff from the BBC's aborted Arabic TV channel, JSC broadcasts debates with the vilified opposition, the views of outlawed political groups and tackles women's rights, torture and polygamy with a liberality denied other print and broadcast organisations. But there's more to JSC than mere fanfares.

Rashid Ghanoushi, exiled leader of the Tunisian opposition party *An-Nahda*, experienced the channel's double standards first hand. Two years ago, Ghanoushi was invited onto JSC's weekly *Sharia al-Hayat* programme to represent the voice of democratic Islam. A couple of minutes into transmission, the programme was cut. He discovered later that Tunis had contacted Sheikh Hamad, the Emir of

Qatar, who pulled the plug. But Ghanoushi still considers JSC 'the best Arab channel', largely because it treats its viewers more seriously.

In flagship programmes like *More Than One Opinion, The Opposing Direction*, and *Confidential*, JSC has hosted a Moroccan official arguing with the Polisario Front; banned opposition groups from Algeria and Syria; and the ostracised Egyptian scholar Nasr Abu Zeid explaining how Quranic textual criticism does not belittle Islam (*Index 4/96*). Saad al-Faqih of the Movement for Islamic Reform in Arabia says JSC has an educational mission in the Middle East. 'As people adjust to no longer being kept in the dark, they become more demanding and their leaders are forced to address the issues they previously sought to hide.'

The rise of critical TV has not been without diplomatic cost: Lebanon is the only Arab state so far not to have filed a complaint about some or other aspect of programme content. And Ghanoushi's experience shows how diplomatic concerns can still outweigh the Emir's tentative patronage of critical discourse. While Saudi exile Mohammed al-Masari sometimes gets a mention and, in June, JSC screened a one-hour profile of the alleged terrorist Usama bin Ladin, no real platform has ever been extended to Saudi dissidents. Similarly, at home, in spite of Sheikh Hamad's democratisation of municipal elections and the enfranchisement of women, the closest JSC has come to representing domestic dissent was a round-table discussion of the 1998

economic summit at Doha.
Neil Sammonds

● **A tangled web** Internet censorship legislation, already through the Australian Senate and almost certain to clear the House of Representatives in the next few weeks threatens to make Australia a no-go area for web users. The legislation, the most draconian to date in the developed world, will take effect on 1 January 2000.

'Internet Services Providers: the Broadcasting Services Amendment (Online Services) Bill 1999' applies an existing film and video classification scheme to net content on the grounds that the internet is like pay television and should be regulated accordingly. It will be administered by the Australian Broadcasting Authority, already responsible for regulating television content.

ISPs will be required to take down prohibited content hosted within Australia and to block access to it if located overseas. X-rated and RC-rated material (non-violent erotica and material that 'offends against the standards of morality, decency and propriety generally accepted by reasonable adults' and material that 'instructs' in matters of crime or violence) is to be prohibited, along with R-rated content (depictions of drug use, nudity and a wide range of other 'adult themes') that is not protected by an adult verification system.

The proposals have been criticised by the industry, civil liberties and user lobby groups and the media, as well as by the political opposition. The government, however, is determined to go ahead.

With a budget of A\$1.5m a year for classification fees (from the Office of Film and Literature Classification, which operates on a cost-recovery scheme), there is no hope that more than a fraction of the content on the net can be classified. However, Senator Alston, the minister responsible for the legislation, is proposing the use of filtering software that could result in great swathes of content being crudely wiped out. While the bill does not specify any such solutions, leaving it to ISPs to take 'reasonable steps' to prevent Australians accessing banned content, there are widespread concerns over the 'collateral damage' that could result from their implementation.

The legislation indemnifies ISPs against any legal proceedings by users that may result as a consquence of their enforcement of its directives.

Foolproof blocking of websites is not easy – it's often said that the internet treats censorship as damage, and works around it – but there is little doubt that implementation of the legislation as proposed would limit access for most users. However, as earlier experiments by Australia's neighbours in the region – Singapore and China for instance – have shown, the machinations of government are no match for the ingenuity of serious netheads. ❑
Danny Yee

OBITUARIES

JIM ROSE (1909 – 1999), trustee of *Index* and Writers and Scholars Educational Trust from 1986 until a few months before his death. His life reflected his many talents and interests, but freedom of speech, like racial equality, was particularly close to his heart. He was the founding director of the International Press Institute, promoting press freedom across the world at the height of the Cold War.

He was a remarkable trustee – an unusually attentive listener, hardworking, courteous, generous, always present at meetings, interested in the staff, meticulous about reading the papers. I took over the editorship at a troubled time for the magazine, and Jim's concern and commitment were demonstrated again and again, his extremely pertinent questions combined with unfailing support. He understood the importance of financial viability in a world where many people believe that good intentions are enough; and he was always the first to write to us when he liked an issue of the magazine or we won a prize. Everyone at *Index* loved him. We shall miss him greatly. ❏ *UO*

EQBAL AHMED (1933 – 1999), political activist and historian, died in Islamabad, Pakistan, on 11 May. His attachment to radical politics began early: while a student at Princeton University he joined the Algerian Liberation Front and supported their fight against France; his outspoken opposition to the Vietnam war led to his arrest and trial on a trumped-up charge of plotting to kidnap Henry Kissinger. Eqbal emerged as one of the most original and provocative analysts of the post-imperial world. His writing on the subject was compelling, eminently readable and thought-provoking.

The last few years of his life were spent in Pakistan. He returned in 1995 with the determination to do what he could to help arrest that country's headlong descent into a dangerous brew of sectarianism, militarism and reactionary Islam. Most notably, this took the form of an attempt to create a new University Khalduniyah – named after his hero, the great Muslim historian Ibn-Khaldun. Successive Pakistani governments chose to thwart the enterprise, fearing the threat it represented to their coercive, narrow-minded ideology. Through his columns, Eqbal continued to promote better relations between India – where he was born and to which he remained much attached – and Pakistan. He died before he could witness the ignominy of Pakistan's latest Kashmiri adventure. ❏ *AA*

MARK FISHER

Keeping shtum

Far from extending the public's right to know, the new Freedom of Information bill offers some additional and imaginitive ways of maintaining secrecy

When a train crashes or a ferry sinks, when there is an outbreak of food poisoning or allegations of police corruption, people want to know the facts. In a democracy they should have the right to know.

In Britain we have never had any legal rights to such information. The government and public bodies release forests of data every day, but they do so by grace and favour, retaining the right to withhold anything that might cause them embarrassment.

Now at last after years of campaigning Britain has a draft 'Freedom of Information bill' with the prospect of legislation next year. In it 'the scales are weighted decisively in favour of openness', claims the Home Secretary, Jack Straw. He says: 'It will radically change the relationship between the government and its citizens.'

However, the Campaign for Freedom of Information calls it 'deeply disappointing' and its co-chairman, James Cornford, fears that it is so ill-conceived that it could become 'as notorious and disreputable as the 1911 Official Secrets Act'. Who is right?

Freedom of information legislation ought to pass three tests. Will it empower the citizen? Will it ensure the release of information which ought to be available in the public interest? Will it avoid or resolve major public crises, and obviate the need for investigations like the Scott Inquiry?

The draft bill sails through the first test. People will at last have a legal right to see what information about them is held by public bodies, such as the police, health authorities, public sector employers, the Benefits Agency, Inland Revenue, and by private bodies carrying out public contracts or functions. This new right will be enforced by an information commissioner who will have powers to adjudicate on complaints and to require compliance with the legislation. Fees for accessing information will be modest.

At last people such as the disabled who have felt themselves powerless when confronted by the wall of bureaucracy will be able to regain a measure of control over their lives.

It is when you start to apply the second and third tests that anxieties begin to crowd in as the bill constructs a hedge of exemptions, exclusions and gateway provisions that limit and inhibit the new statutory right of access.

All FOI bills have the same basic exemptions: national security, defence and international relations, anything that would prevent the police or public prosecutors enforcing the law, protection for personal privacy and commercial confidentiality and policy formulation within government. These recognise that, in practice, all states need to keep some information to themselves. But it is crucial how they are drafted and what checks and balances are built in if such exemptions are not to be an invitation to official abuse.

In the draft bill some of these exemptions are drawn too widely and some are too cautious. Crucially the tests that should be applied when deciding whether exempt information should be withheld or released, the 'harm tests', are too weighted against disclosure even of uncontroversial material.

Clause 25 sensibly exempts access to information whose release would undermine an investigation or prosecution but, instead of time limiting such a block, publication is prevented for all time even if the investigation or prosecution is abandoned or completed. So although the management of the police will be open to scrutiny, the bill will prevent the release of any information about the handling of a murder investigation, such as the death of Stephen Lawrence. The Macpherson Inquiry report recommended that there should be no class exemption for the police.

Sub-clauses specify that this block on investigations applies to the causes of accidents, health and safety at work, and to allegations of mismanagement or misconduct. So reports on accidents such as those involving the *Herald of Free Enterprise* ferry or *The Marchioness* Thames pleasure boat, or inquiries into outbreaks of E. coli poisoning, or investigations into radiation leaks at nuclear plants, will be permanently locked away unless the authorities choose to publish them. As will information about possible breaches of the law on environmental health, racial discrimination and animal welfare.

A total exemption is extended to decision-making and policy formulation in government. All other countries exempt this, but Australia, the Netherlands and Ireland require the disclosure of the factual information and the scientific and technical advice on which policies are based. Without that it is hard to have intelligent public debate and impossible to judge whether government has acted wisely or efficiently. The draft bill prohibits government departments from even confirming or denying the existence of such information. We will have no right to know what advice the government received on BSE or on GM foods.

All this suggests that the government and its officials remain fundamentally suspicious of openness. Yet they have before them the examples of comparable legislation in Australia, Canada and New Zealand, countries that have broadly similar political and judicial systems. In each of these, FOI legislation was passed in the early 1980s so we can see what does and does not work and what are the costs of administering such legislation. British government officials have visited these countries during the past 10 years and it was this experience which informed the drafting of David Clark's White Paper 'Your Right to Know', that preceded this bill.

Furthermore, some ministers, now with two years' experience of government, are beginning to see the benefits of releasing previously withheld information. Jack Straw released the statistics on deaths and suicides in prisons, gaining much credit and contributing to a better quality of debate on prison reform.

In spite of this, the government clearly remains anxious. These exemptions and harm tests would seem to provide a substantial protection for the state from unwanted scrutiny. However, the draft bill offers some additional and imaginative ways of maintaining secrecy.

In other FOI legislation, information that is not exempt may be withheld if the authorities can demonstrate that its release would be undesirable. These harm tests typically range from 'substantial harm' through 'harm', 'endanger', 'damage', to 'adverse effect', 'injury' or 'prejudice'. The White Paper set the test at 'substantial harm'. In contrast, the draft bill tailors each test to the nature of the exemption but opts in almost every case for 'prejudice', the weakest and least precise test. The police and law-enforcement bodies will be subject to no harm test at all, not even having to demonstrate prejudice.

A public authority will be able to insist on knowing why information is being sought and the use to which it will be put, and will then be able, if it chooses, to refuse access or prohibit publication. Innocuous information may be withheld if, when combined with other information that is exempt, its disclosure would cause harm.

Tucked away in Clause 44 of the draft bill is a subsection that allows public authorities to refuse to release information that might expose them to prosecution. This is bizarre. A prime purpose of FOI is to expose wrongdoing. It stands sense on its head that a public body suspected of racial discrimination, pollution or corruption can keep any evidence secret and indeed refuse to cooperate if the information commissioner investigates.

To counteract the reluctance of public authorities to release information, other countries incorporate a strong and independent arbitration system and a binding public interest test into their FOI laws. Publication is required if, on balance, the interests of the public outweigh any possible harm that disclosure might cause.

The draft bill gives powers of adjudication to the commissioner and powers of enforcement but Clause 45 directly prohibits the information commissioner from ordering the publication of information that is being withheld under Clause 14, covering discretionary disclosures.

This mesh of constraints would already appear to be sufficiently fine to prevent any inappropriate openness but, as final safety nets, the draft bill gives the force of law to a minister's 'reasonable opinion' that disclosure of information could 'prejudice the effective conduct of public affairs'. Ministers will also be allowed to introduce additional exemptions by order. British governments publish reams of information every day. Almost all such information is released not because the law requires it or because the public has a basic civil right to know but because ministers permit it. To legislate for the release of government information through the gateway of a minister's 'reasonable opinion' is, like dear Henry, to return to the hole in the bucket.

Why is this draft bill so unnecessarily timid and anxious? The Labour Party in opposition had a long-standing and detailed commitment to legislate. Both John Smith and Tony Blair made repeated public declarations of support. In 1996 Blair said, 'It is not some isolated constitutional reform that we are proposing with a FOI Act. It is a change that is absolutely fundamental to how we see politics developing in this country over the next few years.' It was this spirit that informed the White Paper.

When responsibility for this was moved in July 1998 from the Cabinet Office to the Home Office there was a fundamental change in approach. Whereas the White Paper began from a presumption of openness and saw FOI as a civil right, the Home Office seems to have started from a belief that public information is the intellectual property of the authority that created it. It is inevitable that those who see information as intellectual property will come to a different judgement on the desirability of openness to those who see it as a civil right.

The reality is that few ministers in this government see FOI as a priority and few believe that it will strengthen government. Many are convinced that it will make the hard job of governing more difficult – the attitude of ministers and civil servants in successive British governments.

These are outdated attitudes rooted in fear and buttressed by ignorance. The experience of other comparable democracies, almost all of which have FOI legislation, is that being open improves the quality of decision-making in government.

It is not too late to strengthen this draft bill. It has been published as a 'Consultation on Draft Legislation'. Representations can be made by writing to MPs or directly to the official responsible for this consultation: Stephen Winter. The bill will be scrutinised by select committees in the Commons and the Lords.

The bill is likely to feature in the 1999/2000 legislative programme and will then be debated by both houses and considered in committee, when detailed amendments can be tabled.

The quality of that consultation and scrutiny will determine whether, at last, people in Britain will have the right to know. ❑

Mark Fisher *is MP for Stoke-on-Trent. He introduced the Right To Know bill in 1993.*
Representations can be made to MPs or to Stephen Winter, Home Office, 50 Queen Anne's Gate, London, SW1H 9AT – fax 0171 -273 2684, or consultation.foi.ho@gtnet.gov.uk by 20 July 1999.

ANDY WASLEY

Spiking dissent

Across Europe, reporting direct action and promoting dissenting viewpoints has led both mainstream and alternative media into conflict with the law

Just before 7am on Thursday 13 April, Martin Hager, a journalist based in Frankfurt am Rhein, Germany, had his door kicked down by five intruders. Believing he was about to be robbed, he tried to phone the police, only to discover the five men were the police. They had come to seize his computers, research notes, video camera, tapes and contacts diary, and to arrest him for 'producing material likely to incite disorder'.

Hager had been working on a number of video documentaries and articles questioning NATO's bombing campaign in the Balkans and urging the public to demand a referendum on Germany's participation. His articles had encouraged direct action protests. The police had other ideas. Although Hager is still waiting to be formally charged, none of his possessions have been returned and deadlines have come and gone. Opposition to NATO attacks has become the latest victim of a growing tendency towards overt and covert news management across Europe.

A report due later this year, *Banned: the real state of media in Europe today* finds 'politically motivated' censorship is becoming an 'extensive' problem across the continent. It lists 'literally hundreds' of examples of censorship, primarily the suppression of material deemed 'inappropriate for public consumption'. Although the primary target so far has been the alternative press, mainstream outlets that cover dissenting views on environmental, social and political issues have come under fire.

The conviction of the editors of *Green Anarchist* magazine for 'conspiracy to incite criminal damage' in November 1997 (*Index* 1/98) put 'political' censorship back on the media map and hinted that a wider crackdown on the alternative press was likely. In the months immediately before and after the case, a number of European publications similar to

Green Anarchist were targeted and, in some cases, closed down. In early 1998, *Ravage,* a Dutch environmental magazine, was raided, its editors arrested for alleged 'incitement to cause illegal damage' and a significant amount of written material seized. Charges were never brought but, despite the support of the Dutch Association of Journalists, *Ravage* failed to recover any of the material that had been seized.

The first raid on *Ravage* came only weeks after a meeting of European intelligence agencies in the UK to discuss the future of 'Europol' – the multinational police force primarily designed to gather information on organised crime in Europe, but whose remit also includes the monitoring of subversive groups and publications. Within days of the attack on *Ravage*'s Amsterdam office, environmental journalists in France were arrested for producing a newsletter and video documentary examining the issues surrounding the country's road-building scheme. All copies of the video were confiscated and the newsletter 'halted' at the printers. According to eyewitnesses, at least one of the security service officers present was Dutch.

A week later, journalists connected to *Radikal,* a German publication with a progressive position on the environment and social justice, were raided for the fifth time. It has been forced to transfer most of its news coverage on to the Internet to avoid interference at the printers. Journalists present were reportedly questioned about their possible relationship with *Ravage* and other environmental publications. Some months later, in early 1997, activists and journalists involved in the UK 'Anti-Election' protest were detained and questioned by plain-clothes police about the production of a newspaper suggesting that the general election had been cancelled. All 20,000 copies of their paper – *Evading Standards,* a pun on London's popular *Evening Standard* – were seized at the printers and pulped. One of the officers questioning the activists informed them: '[Your] colleagues in Europe are already behind bars.'

Although the evidence may suggest an organised, Europe-wide crackdown on the alternative press, Hugh Lawrence, a journalist investigating abuses of press freedom in Europe, believes this has more to do with the wider changes taking place in western Europe. 'All these countries are experiencing a dramatic rise in the number of dissenting voices and in the number of people taking direct action ... It's an over-statement to assume that there is some all-powerful Euro-censor; each country is simply dealing with the perceived threat in its own manner, even if this means borrowing techniques from neighbouring countries.

Lawrence also claims that the growth of selective news suppression has more to do with specific issues than with an all-out attack on campaigning groups. Consequently, the number of mainstream media outlets being intimidated or harassed is on the increase. 'Established press organisations are being regularly threatened or censored for covering issues that the authorities do not want publicised,' he says. In Germany and Finland, for instance, TV and radio programmes on animal rights activists have been pulled at the last minute; journalists in Poland, Norway, Austria and the UK have had similar problems (*Index* 5/98).

Extreme right-wing publications have also excited the interest of the would-be political censors. In addition to their long-term bans on the writing, transmission or distribution of neo-Nazi and anti-Semitic material, the authorities in several European countries have recently stepped up their harassment of any media outlet publishing these views: over 26 journalists and media outlets have run into trouble for giving space to neo-Nazi groups. This could be because of fears over racial violence associated with the increasing numbers of refugees arriving in Europe. In Germany, for instance, the offices of an internet news provider, True Word, were recently raided, research material taken and the editors detained for allowing a neo-Nazi spokesman to take part in an online discussion. Although no criminal charges have been brought, True Word was offline for nearly three weeks.

Professional bodies such as the UK's National Union of Journalists (NUJ) are often reluctant to act on cases where the distinction between 'journalists' and 'activists' becomes blurred. But for Paul O'Connor of Undercurrents, the video news collective, it's much more straightforward. 'Often the only way journalists can cover an event properly is to put themselves in the firing line. If you're covering a road protest, you need to be up in the trees. If that breaks the law as defined by the police on the day and you get arrested, the official bodies still have a duty to protect that individual. News coverage from behind a wire fence half a mile away from the action is simply playing into the hands of the news managers.' ❏

Andy Wasley is a journalist and researcher specialising in media issues. He is editor of a fortnightly news journal, The Brighton and Hove People

JULIAN PETLEY

Dishing the dirt

Satellite television is synonymous with Murdoch and the homogenised monoculture of BskyB. But it doesn't have to be like that: take Med-TV for instance

Med-TV is a Kurdish-language satellite television station funded by investors from Kurdish communities in Europe. It began broadcasting from London in May 1995, although its production centre is in Brussels. Serving the world's largest stateless nation – 35m people scattered throughout Europe, North Africa and the Middle East, the majority in Turkey – Med's schedule is a broad mix of cultural, educational, entertainment and news programmes, 90 per cent produced in-house. As managing director Hikmet Tabak says, 'Med-TV is a wonderful example of how the satellite technology of the modern world, often seen as an implement for abolishing cultural differences, can also be a tool for preserving them.'

Not any more. Med has been forced off the air. Because it broadcast from Britain, Med had to be licensed by the Independent Television Commission (ITC) and obey its Programme Code. On 23 April, the ITC revoked Med's licence; the station had breached the Commission's clauses on impartiality and incitement to violence. The crucial question is, of course, whether a code designed for broadcasters in a democracy can and should be applied to a station operating under very different circumstances. Much of Med's audience lives in Turkey where, as Article 19's *State Before Freedom: Media Repression in Turkey* concludes, 'freedom of expression remains severely curtailed'.

The ITC monitors compliance with its code and investigates complaints from viewers. In March 1996, it upheld a complaint that, during the December 1995 election campaign in Turkey, Med had given regular and positive coverage to HADEP (the party most sympathetic to the Kurds) and very little to the others. Med pointed out that other parties had been invited to participate but had refused. Tabak complained at the time: 'Our opponents are working to Middle Eastern rules, but we have to abide by British standards.'

In November 1996, the ITC ruled against two further programmes – although no complaint had been received. The first was a news item which included a posthumous statement by a suicide bomber sympathetic to the Workers' Party of Kurdistan (PKK). The ITC argued that the presenter made no distinction between the general Kurdish point of view and that of the PKK, interpreting this as partiality. It also felt that the presenter's comments were 'difficult to reconcile' with the code's requirements on incitement. A second programme, a documentary illustrating life in a PKK base, 'concluded with a shot of, and quotation from, the leader of the PKK which could have implied the licensee's endorsement of his party'. Med accepted that mistakes had been made, but pointed out that the news item had coincided with the sudden withdrawal of Med's satellite capacity (see below), which contributed to a 'lack of editorial vigilance'. The ITC issued a formal warning that further breaches could result in the suspension, revocation even, of Med's licence.

In January 1998, the ITC fined Med £90,000 (US$145,000) for three breaches of the code's impartiality requirements. On 14 June 1997, the ITC found a programme on a PKK rally lacking in contextual or balancing material. A news item on 9 October condemned a US list of proscribed terrorist organisations that included the PKK; the ITC felt that Med endorsed the condemnation. Again, on 3 June, the ITC criticised a news item that described members of the Kurdish Democratic Party as 'murderous and treacherous'.

In June 1998, the ITC issued another formal warning following a 55-minute interview with Semdin Sakik, a commander in ARGK, the PKK's military wing, in which he anticipated an expansion of the guerrilla war into Turkey and beyond. The item had been broadcast on 14 October 1997 and there had been no complaints, but the ITC said Sakik's remarks constituted incitement to violence and were not 'balanced' by a critical comment from the interviewer. The ITC warned it might revoke Med's licence if further incidents occurred.

There followed two more breaches and a complaint. In March 1998, the politician Mehmet Sah, employed as a news reporter, expressed personal views that the ITC felt condoned self-immolation, as had *Pazar Sohbeti* (Sunday Forum) a month earlier. Med pointed out its difficulties in placing correspondents in Turkey due to the hostility of the government: Sah had been used because no one else was available. The station also argued that it had not condoned suicide but merely tried to explain its significance in Kurdish culture. Unimpressed, the ITC now required Med to provide it with a monthly log of all news and documentary programmes, detailing the participants involved, their political affiliations and the airtime allocated.

On 22 March this year, the ITC suspended Med's licence for 21 days. Crucial here were statements by PKK and ARGK representatives in Med news reports after the arrest of PKK leader Abdullah Oçalan, statements the ITC felt contained 'calls to direct violence and criminal actions of various kinds'. Following its suspension, Med proposed a number of reforms. These included reducing the amount of live broadcasting; shortening news programmes; placing greater responsibility on producers to ensure code compliance; raising standards of professionalism; and devoting more of the schedule to educational, cultural and entertainment programmes. On 9 April, Med and its legal advisers Stephens Innocent made formal representations to the ITC. They were unsuccessful. On 23 April, Med's licence was permanently revoked. ITC chairman Sir Robin Biggam said: 'It is not in the public interest to have any broadcaster use the UK as a platform for broadcasts which incite people to violence.'

From its beginnings, Med faced intense harassment from the Turkish government. Its first weapon was disinformation: it labelled Med 'PKK TV', a term that was picked up by reputable publications such as *Screen Digest* and the *Independent*. In Turkey, Med's viewers were harassed, detained and tortured. In April 1995, foreign minister Erdal Inonu wrote to the British embassy in Ankara asking for Med's licence to be revoked. In the same month, *New Media Markets* claimed that after the Turkish government complained to the UK foreign office, it had asked the ITC to close down Med. In October, the foreign office cut off Med's free daily satellite news feed.

Off the record, foreign office officials briefed that Med was an 'irritant' whose relationship with the PKK was concealed by 'green baize doors'. Between May and June 1995, the Turkish authorities asked the

ITC three times to investigate the ownership, licensing and content of
Med. During a visit in November 1995, Prime Minister Tansu Ciller
presented John Major with a dossier in support of her request that Med
be banned. A month later, she asked the German government to ban
Med's cable broadcasts. In the same month, its signal was jammed during
a live debate involving Oçalan; and in January 1996, the Turkish daily
Yeni Yuzyil reported that the general directorate for wireless
communications had completed research that showed it was feasible to
jam Med's signals from sites in Turkey.

The following July, Turkish pressure on the Polish national
telecommunications agency led to Med losing its place on Eutelsat's
communication transponders; it was forced off the air until new capacity
could be found. Med approached BT, among others. This resulted in
further pressure on the British government. Broadcasting deals with
Intelsat and Orion also collapsed following Turkish pressure. In
September 1996, Med's offices in London and Brussels were raided by
police looking for material linking it to terrorism. Computers, disks and
files were seized and 80 staff were arrested, although no charges were
brought. In 1997, Med was jammed for three weeks, and again for three
days in October 1998.

The Turkish embassy in London confirmed that, during the events
leading up to the revocation of Med's licence, it had made a submission
to the ITC, which subsequently admitted it had been lobbied by Istanbul
(as well as by thousands of Kurds). The foreign office said it supported
the ITC's decision – though stressed that the commission had acted
independently. Nor should the above catalogue, which illustrates the
immense pressures exerted by the Turkish government on anyone
remotely associated with Med, be taken as suggesting otherwise.

In the circumstances, however, was it wise of Sir Robin Biggam not
to absent himself from the ITC's deliberations on Med? He is, after all, a
non-executive director of British Aerospace, which is about to start
licensed production in Turkey of assault rifles and grenades for the
security services. ❏

*Julian Petley is a lecturer in media and communication studies at Brunel
University*

South Africa: the morning after

Credit: Benny Gool/Trace Image

The ANC's election victory in June fell one seat short of the two-thirds majority needed to change South Africa's Constitution, one of the most progressive on the continent. Not that President Thabo Mbeki wants to – not yet. But the · country is in the midst of a crime wave of staggering dimensions and Nelson Mandela's era of reconciliation has come to an end. The ground has shifted since the disappearance of white government five years ago, but in some areas of life it's not much and not always for the better. ❏

MICHAEL GRIFFIN

The way it is

South Africa's latest drama caused a storm when it hit small screens in February. But the real triumph was that township life could look and sound as snappy as *NYPD* or *Homicide: Life on the Streets*

A teacher shoots himself in class, a girl is raped between lessons, boys smoke *dagga* in the lavatories and Papa Action sells it in the yard – thanks to the compliant headmaster.

This is everyday life in the township school depicted in the South
African Broadcasting Corporation (SABC) serial, *Yizo Yizo* ('The way it
is'). First aired in February, the 13-part serial achieved cult status among
young blacks for its gritty approach to township realities. It won the
largest viewing figures in broadcasting history and stirred a nationwide
debate on censorship in time for the national elections.

'In the eyes of South African parents, these things just don't happen
in our schools,' said GA Hill, news editor at Johannesburg radio station,
YFM. 'No one gets shot, no one gets raped, kids don't give in to peer
pressure, teenage pregnancies do not occur and kids don't contract HIV.
Yizo Yizo is the wake-up call.'

Most of the controversy surrounding the series stemmed from
supposed 'copycat' incidents. In one school, a bully forced another
pupil's head down the lavatory and flushed, apparently out of the sheer
joy at reproducing a scene from *Yizo Yizo*. In another, pupils sacked a
classroom and tried to set it on fire to cries of '*Yizo Yizo*'. In April, a
Soweto principal was robbed and shot to death in her office by youths.
The attack was described as '*Yizo Yizo*-like' by a white-dominated
media hungry for proof that the series incited black secondary school
students to violence and should, therefore, be taken off air.

Set against the flood of high profile rapes and killings that have made
South Africans more tolerant than ever of police brutality to suspects,
Yizo Yizo gave the better-off a glimpse into the pit where their security
fears germinate – the nearest township. Novelist Mandla Langa, the
newly-appointed chairman of the Independent Broadcasting Authority
and former ANC representative in London, told the *Sowetan* in April
that the debate about whether screen violence is a reflection of the ills of
society, or whether it contributes to making people more brutal, had
become acute in South Africa. But he refused to give in to demands for
Yizo Yizo to be banned. 'The violence is not gratuitous,' he stone-
walled.

At the heart of *Yizo Yizo* lies a simple morality tale of the old and
new South Africas. It explores the collapse of Supatsela High after the
cane-wielding principal Mr Mthembu is forced to leave after brutally
assaulting a pupil. Mthembu had ruled with fear instead of instilling a
sense of self-discipline and responsibility in the students. The principal
who follows allows the school to degenerate into a playground for petty
criminals and drug-dealers. He is eventually replaced by a new and feisty

woman principal who, with a small group of teachers, students and members of the community, manages to turn the school around. '*Yizo* shows what is happening,' continued Langa, 'but goes further to show that community action can deal with violence and that even the most feared and hardened gangsters can be routed through community action.'

Made by the Laduma Film Factory and co-financed by SABC and the Education Department, shooting was preceded by a six-week period of research via focus groups with teachers, students and parents. The key findings to emerge included: the high incidence of drug and alcohol abuse in schools; attitudes condoning rape and sexual abuse; the powerlessness felt by teachers since the abolition of corporal punishment; the endless delays around rationalisation and redeployment; and the breakdown in relationships between teachers and pupils – who tend to blame each other for the crisis in schools.

But the real revelation for most viewers was how electric life could be made to seem at the bottom of the heap. *Yizo*'s two directors, Angus Gibson – known for his work on the 'tracking' series *7 Up* and *14 Up* – and the young Tebogo Mahalatsi, use stock which gives nuance to the glare of township life, a fast editing rhythm, acres of *kwaito* music and a tapestry of characters speaking a patois of Afrikaans, Zulu and Xhosa – and none of them white. That's the way it is, away from the bulk of SABC's programming.❏

Michael Griffin with South African sources

NTHABISENG MOGALE

Best-kept secret

South African women are living on the front-line of a war in which one of them is raped every 12 seconds. It wasn't like that before black rule, the whites say. Or was it?

The rape rate in South Africa has always been extraordinarily high. I grew up in a small township west of Johannesburg. My family was unfortunate in that we were allocated a house directly across from the graveyard. I lost count of how many times I was woken by screams in the night from women being violated in the dark. Cemeteries, like most other public areas, were never serviced by township governments, in spite of the high rents we paid, until the 1980s boycotts.

The community intervened in my township, but their measures placed a further burden on women. You were reprimanded for travelling at night, for being by yourself, keeping the 'wrong company' or dressing in a provocative manner. The responsibility of the National Party government to provide security for all citizens was never discussed. Well-lit roads, manicured parks and police patrols were a white privilege that blacks would never dare ask for. The government wasn't interested in rape: women were discouraged from reporting it, arrests were rare and, in the few townships where statistics were kept, they were never readily available. When People Opposing Women Abuse (POWA) was formed 20 years ago, it was sidelined as a pressure group that focused on a 'marginal' feminist issue.

Besides, what point was there in reporting a crime the police had never been trained to deal with? The duties of the township officers were to keep tabs on 'comrades and communists'. Other crimes did not warrant attention, either from the public services or the media. South Africa was a 'Christian country' with a few communists seeking to render it ungovernable, but even they were 'under control'. All was well.

Secrecy about crimes other than political was the norm. The censorship of sexual crimes reached a peak.

Journalists who write that South Africa has become the rape capital of the world fail to compare today's statistics with those of 10 years ago. This is not because there was no rape 10 years ago, merely no statistics. The lack of community organisation against rape in the past helped to keep the crime underground. In the 1980s, the white government had commandeered rape as a means to intimidate women activists. We heard the testimony of the '1 Million' and 'Makabasa' gangs at the Truth and Reconciliation Commission (TRC). They were set up in Soweto and Welkom and Parys in the Orange Free State, specifically to kidnap and gang-rape young women in a form of violence known as 'jackrolling'.

The jackrollers' crimes have never been fully documented, despite attempts by survivors to make themselves heard. Even women activists, who had been raped by their comrades and then raped again by police in detention, refused to break their silence. To talk about their violation would have given the enemy an opportunity to divide them. We had to close ranks.

The TRC held hearings that were specifically intended to address the suffering that women experienced during the apartheid era. Among those lining up to bear witness were women who had held high positions in the liberation movement. Their testimony could have paved the way for other women to speak publicly, to bring rape to the fore, without feeling uncomfortable. None of those violations were revealed, robbing us of a chance to understand crimes against women, irrespective of the perpetrator. It is a missed opportunity that POWA will forever regret.

The 'new' South Africa ratified the Convention on the Elimination of All Forms of Discrimination Against Women, developed one of the most progressive constitutions in the world and assembled a government more than a quarter of whose MPs were women. Women took a leadership role in a manner unprecedented in South Africa or the rest of the world. But these landmarks occurred against the backdrop of a youth that was increasingly branded as a 'lost generation'. Most had had no formal education since the mid-1980s when they were scarcely teenagers. They had no skills to sell in a sharply narrowed job market. Their only means of communication was the violence society had used and legitimised over the years. It humiliated them and forced them to conform. Today they use it to force women to conform.

Policing structures are only now being rebuilt and pressure on government to deal with other crimes has affected their capacity to cope with rape. A hostile justice system compounds the problem. Magistrates feel overwhelmed at having to deal with a problem based on its legal, rather than political, merits. This is why there are still discrepancies in the sentencing of perpetrators. Rape against blacks is still not taken as seriously as rape against whites. There were 38 reported rapes in the rich suburb of Sandton in the first half of 1998, compared to 271 in Alexandra township. The two districts are separated by less than 5 km. The survivors' trauma has been given a defiant and articulate voice in testimony from journalist Charlene Smith, gender commissioner and MP's wife Nomboniso Gasa and a UN official, all of whom were raped recently. But, if you are black, 20 and living in a township, you need to be gang-raped by 30 men and left for dead to win similar media attention.

Now it is common to hear about rape on the midday news bulletin. Unfortunately this openness takes place in a society that is racially divided and it conforms to the us–and–them culture which has been nurtured for decades. Most rapes are perpetrated by black men, although the majority of survivors are also black. White people put up higher walls, install more alarms, extra immobilisers for their cars and trade horror stories at the drop of a hat. They cannot understand why a police station cannot be built on their corner immediately. They do not understand that their domestic workers who travel through dark alleys or aboard unlit trains in the early morning are at far greater risk than they. It is not that rape has increased beyond all imagining, only that the mammoth task of levelling the playing field for all South Africans means that the well-protected white population takes a fairer share of the risks faced by their black neighbours. ❏

Nthabiseng Mogale is director of People Opposing Women Abuse (POWA) *which provides counselling for rape survivors, public education, shelters for abused women and their children, lobbying, advocacy and economic empowerment*

MAX DU PREEZ

White pebble, black shoe

Proximity to power can be a dangerous thing, particularly for good journalism

Journalists through the ages share a common weakness: the temptation
to be close to the powerful. It's understandable. On the social scale we
rank somewhere below used car salesmen. We work with powerful
people all the time, but are made constantly aware of our low standing.

There are few things more flattering to the average journalist than to
be invited to a social occasion by a politician, businessman or celebrity.
Journalists love telling each other about parties or the confidential
conversations they had there with the people in power.

Understandable it may be, but it is the enemy of good journalism. It
was what made the South African Broadcasting Corporation (SABC)
such a powerful tool of the apartheid regime. Senior SABC journalists
defined their worth according to their closeness to National Party
cabinet ministers or the police and army generals.

After the advent of democracy in 1994, the SABC returned to being
a public, rather than a state, broadcaster. Within four years, the entire top
echelon of the corporation became almost totally black, instead of 100
per cent white. Stories of the people of South Africa, rather than the
views of the white supremacist elite, filled news bulletins and
documentaries. It was a Prague Spring, sadly, that lasted barely five years.

Towards the end of 1998, old patterns began to return. A group of
senior news managers started concentrating power in their own hands.
Their boasts are not of the great stories they broke, but at whose party
they have been, or what confidences Thabo Mbeki had shared with
them. They define their worth by their access to the ANC's inner circle.

The government's stand on media freedom was repeated publicly and

often in the run-up to the June elections. But the cynical view now is
that the ruling party can afford to feel comfortable about the SABC,
because there is a cabal of loyalists at the top who will never need
direction. They anticipate what the ruling elite wants and then broadcast
it. It is a step worse than self-censorship.

One problem is that the new news managers are not experienced
journalists. The new South African reality dictates that management
should be black but, because of decades of apartheid, there is a critical
shortage of experienced black journalists, especially ones with broadcast
experience. (Although the most senior black journalist, Joe Thloloe, was
editor of TV news at SABC until the same cabal got rid of him.)

TV and radio news at SABC are now run by four people. The top
man is 36-years-old. A print journalist for a few years, he worked for the
new government before becoming corporate manager at SABC in 1996.
The number two was a soldier in the ANC's liberation army before
going to Bulgaria where he worked as a journalist.

One cannot blame these guys for feeling insecure about their
qualifications. The news they control on three television channels and
more than a dozen radio stations is the primary source of information
for South Africa. But insecure people with lots of unchecked power
often become arrogant and authoritarian. And this is the point where my
career at the SABC came to an abrupt end on 16 April this year.

I have been around the block a few times in South African
journalism. I was political correspondent for the *Sunday Times* and
Business Day before founding and editing the first anti-apartheid
Afrikaans newspaper, *Vrye Weekblad* (Independent Weekly). It became
the most prosecuted newspaper in South African history for exposing on
a weekly basis state death squads, police torture, chemical warfare and
corruption. It closed in January 1994 after losing a defamation suit
lodged by the head of the SA Police Forensics Unit. Our allegations, that
he had prepared poisons to kill anti-apartheid activists, were eventually
proved before the Truth Commission in 1998.

I joined SABC as a current affairs anchor and documentary producer
two months before the 1994 election. In 1996 I assembled a team which
produced 94 weekly documentaries on the Truth Commission process.
TRC Special Report was watched by millions and swept South Africa's
media awards. When it ended, I launched an investigative documentary
series, *Special Assignment*, which again won many awards.

On 16 April, I was called in and told that my annual contract would not be renewed for the sixth time, 'because I had lost respect for television news management'. Well, perhaps I did, but I never showed it.

It's simple. Since early 1999, the new management undermined all independence and the free flow of ideas inside News and Current Affairs. A man whose only TV experience had been in the news rooms of PW Botha and FW de Klerk, was put in charge. He took the power and initiative away from me as programme editor and executive producer of *Special Assignment*. If he had done it well, it would have been another matter, but he bungled. I questioned and resisted, without ever defying them, but it was enough. I was a threat to the cabal's hegemony; to the increasing drive to turn the whole of SABC into loyal, uniform and uncritical soldiers. I became a pebble in its shoe.

I think these men realise they made a mistake. The issue exploded into a public debate and featured for weeks in newspaper columns and radio talk shows. And that was the positive side of the episode. The fact that most journalists outside SABC – mostly black and progressive – publicly criticised my dismissal (SABC journalists did so privately); that the Media Workers' Association of SA and the South African Union of Journalists joined in a campaign launched by the Friends of the Public Broadcaster and the Freedom of Expression Institute, must tell us that South African civil society will not stand for this kind of abuse of power.

The campaign forced the board to launch an investigation into both editorial independence at the SABC and my own dismissal. The enquiry will conclude at the end of June. I have no reason to suspect that the board is not sincere in its investigation, but I'm afraid the cabal at the helm of radio and TV news is too powerful and well-connected for any finding to force them to change their ways.

A senior Zimbabwean journalist spoke at a gathering in Pretoria on World Press Freedom Day in May. It was the 'sunshine journalism' practised in Zimbabwe after independence that led to the 'present darkness' there, he said. I hope his warning is taken seriously. Our parliamentary opposition is now very, very weak, which means we need an independent, vigorous media more than ever.

But don't hold your breath. ❏

Max du Preez, *veteran anti-apartheid journalist and broadcaster, was 'let go' by the SABC on 16 April 1999*

Tribes

Lawyers denied their humanity, settlers stole their lands, administrators deemed their languages worthless, governments denied their right to nationhood. *Index* **looks at the continuing battle for land and language waged by the world's tribes**

File compiled by Hugh Brody and Ted Chamberlin. From 1996-99, Hugh Brody and Ted Chamberlin, supported by the Connaught Fund at the University of Toronto, have worked together on issues of language and indigenous culture.
Hugh Brody's work in the Kalahari has been supported by Comic Relief.

lands, Canada – Credit: Rex/Komulainen

HUGH BRODY

Taking the words from their mouths

Human beings make about 160 different sounds. This, say the linguists, is the sum of the vocal elements of all the world's languages. English, one of the more complicated vocal systems, has about 55 of these sounds. Norwegian has 75. The Bushman or San languages of the Kalahari have more than 145. In the words of Tony Traill, an expert on southern African linguistics, the San are the great acrobats of the mouth. In their campaigns against tribes, in particular against hunter-gatherers, the colonists have despised them for the very sounds of their voices and, with curious determination, have sought to eradicate their languages. As if the mind of the tribe were itself the enemy.

Throughout the world, there has been a drastic loss of tribal languages. Some linguists estimate that some 5,000 languages or distinctive dialects have faded away this century. In the Americas alone there are more than 1,000 languages that have disappeared or reached the brink of extinction in the past 30 years. With the expansion of schools and other homogenising social processes, the pace of this loss has accelerated; and it continues. The loss of these ways of speaking and of knowing the world is a diminution of the collective human mind: a loss of genius that may well be irrecoverable. It is also a cause of intense grief and disorientation to hundreds of thousands of tribal men and women, who struggle to be themselves without the words to say what that means.

In southern Africa, Dutch settlers dismissed the KhoiSan ways of speaking as 'gibberings of monkeys'. In the forests of India, missionaries noted that much of the language was 'gifted with a clicking, harsh, heavy pronunciation peculiar to all barbaric tongues'. In Australia, aboriginal ways of speaking were often described as 'less than human'. In both the United States and Canada, those concerned to deal with 'the Indian problem' in the nineteenth century resolved that 'those barbaric tongues' would be eradicated, making way for the English that 'all who are civilised can understand'.

Ethnic cleansing and genocide are often said to have been the special curse of the twentieth century. But in their original form, as a war of settlers against tribes, of farmers against hunters, they have been a grim part of the history of human settlement for thousands of years. And ethnic cleansing has been the experience of all the indigenous and tribal peoples wherever agricultural colonialism has advanced. Using steel, horses, germs, guns, courts, churches, schools and parliaments – in whatever combination or sequence worked best for each particular invasion – those in the old world hungry for new lands have invaded the territories of the peoples of the new world. New only to us, of course.

The removal of the great tribes from Georgia in the American southeast was debated, litigated, preached and promoted before they staggered out to the so-called Indian territories of the western plains in what became known as the Trail of Tears. And from the European capitals came instructions to colonial governors that resulted in the laundering and bleaching of the colonies of Africa, Asia, Australia and all the aboriginal domains of the Pacific, as well as every part of the Americas.

The Europeans' assault on tribal languages is well documented; and most persistent when its victims have been hunter-gatherers. These were the tribes whose ways of life meant they were spread far and wide across settlement frontiers. There seems to have been a compulsion to achieve, in these places, a final and decisive silence. Holocaust was not enough; the decimation of population, eradication of whole cultures, relocation of communities from lands the settlers wanted to those they did not, confinement of the survivors of these projects in tiny 'reserves' and 'reservations' and 'homelands' did not achieve a silence that was quite absolute. There were survivors, adults and children who could maintain the traditions, attitudes and idioms of the tribe. The administrators of indigenous lands and societies, the imperial arbiters of tribal fate, sought to put an end to these voices. The sounds of the chattering monkeys, barbaric tongues and less than human vocalisations would cease, to be replaced by English or Spanish, Portuguese, French, Afrikaans: any language of 'civilisation'.

Tribal people often say that to have stories about a land is to own it. The continuing voices, using the languages that carry the stories, that hold the knowledge, that sustain the links with the spirits, are a permanent challenge. A rival title deed to the territory. They must be silenced.

The voices of the tribes of our 'new worlds' contain their own way of owning, knowing and caring for their lands. Their stories are both a form of resistance and a record of what has taken place. Their ways of speaking and their forms of knowledge represent some of the oldest and richest expressions of the human mind. Their silence has a poignancy that reaches deep into the history of the world and the fate of the human mind.

All this means that within many nation states there are ways of life, whole cultures, albeit pressed to the margins of both geography and society, whose existence is shaped by a bitter paradox. On the one hand, these are people whose presence on particular territories reaches back to a time when nation-states did not exist: they are the original, indigenous dwellers and can claim priority and rights that transcend those of all who are relative newcomers to their lands. But they live at political, legal and geographical margins, deprived of many of their richest resources and denied rights to their heritage, if not to life itself. This paradox, the depth of historical claim alongside extreme colonial exploitation, defines the tribal peoples of the world.

In the 1960s, eruptive liberation movements were emerging among tribal peoples and the story of this paradox was being told with new force. In Canada, the great Shuswap leader, George Manuel, coined the expression 'the fourth world' to define a communality of tribal interests. His vision was of emerging nations, not broken communities. The tribes, in his view, were nations within nations and should be recognised as such. But he also said, repeatedly, that the colonial assault upon the fourth world was most clearly to be seen in attacks on cultural heritage and language, both institutional – by missionaries, local government officials and schools – and more subtly subversive as in the racism of frontier settlers and the discriminatory routines of everyday life.

Since the work of Frantz Fanon, intellectuals and activists have been alert to the way in which this combination of racist forces – the institutional and the routine – works its way into the lives and psyche of tribal people. Those who endure protracted colonial oppression internalise the attitudes of those who oppress them. The anger of tribal people is intense, but often directed inward. And they fall into a deep silence.

No wonder, then, that the surviving descendants of these tribes, the men and women whose oral heritages carry the stories as well as the scars of these relentless and merciless events, have an intensely difficult and complicated relationship to their own voices. They often speak the languages of their oppressors and have absorbed the lessons the oppressors have addressed to them: indigenous customs, history and ways of speech are matters of shame. They witness in their daily lives the continuing discrimination and disdain that are shown toward them. So how can they speak? And to whom? Many tribal peoples have survived by remaining hidden, silent and unnoticed, at the remotest margins of the colonial world. They have judged it unsafe or unwise to raise their heads and voices too high above the parapets behind which they have been able to conceal themselves. Who out there is going to listen? Who knows how to listen? So silence is appropriate in many ways. but this silence can also be deep within the psyche as well as a matter of wise strategy. Shame and grief, accumulated from generation to generation, can tie the tongue tight.

Yet the silence, in many parts of the world, is being broken. Land claims movements, cultural revival, anti-colonial protest, a refusal to disappear. Tribal voices are making themselves heard, talking within their families, to their children and grandchildren, about their own lives. Their stories celebrate distinctive kinds of knowledge and speak of everyday events in their own lands. They are assertions of pride and rights: to know their place is to claim it, whatever the colonists might say.

But this is only a glimpse, an echo of the assertion of tribal rights and voices worldwide. We could be hearing from the people of Irian Jaya, who have struggled for a generation against a murderous invasion of their lands and lives by Indonesian settlers and military. In Sri Lanka, the Vaniall-atto, former inhabitants of the entire island now reduced to 2,000 people, are fighting for their rights. In Australia, Aborigine groups are defending every part that remains of their heritage and lands, bringing their stories to the courts as well as to one another. Throughout Latin America, indigenous peoples are raising their voices in order to keep their voices – defying the genocidal process that began with the arrival of the first Europeans and has reduced their numbers and languages by about 90 per cent.

There are many kinds of tribal peoples. Perhaps we can all claim some form of tribal membership, some community to which at times we say we belong that is not our national identity. In many countries there are populations, subcultures, that are stigmatised by a dominant group as dark, unclean and dangerous. These are the 'other' who have the task of defending their heritage and, at times, their very homes against many forms of aggression. They too can be the victims of ethnicide. They include, of course, the people for whose fate the modern expressions 'final solution' and 'ethnic cleansing' were coined. In many ways, and at particular points in their histories, Kosovans, Bosnians, Kurds, Armenians, gypsies and Jews (to name but a few) have suffered brutal forms of prejudice and dispossession. And their voices also have been suppressed. Perhaps they can make common cause with the tribals who live the paradox of earliest claim and least status. Their experiences, and therefore their voices, will sound familiar to all who have dealt in the struggles of indigenous populations.

The resurgence of tribal voice has to do with both land and language. For tribal people, the connections between language and land are self-evident: they have always been there; their knowing these places is inseparable from their economic strength and their right to be there. They are where the battle takes place. From the point of view of settlers and their nation states, these are marginal, infertile territories. (Though some of them now turn out to be rich in minerals, making a new colonial bid for some of the remotest of tribal territories.) They are the lands where tribal peoples have been able to endure, beyond the most aggressive incursions of the colonists. They are languages that somehow 'belong to the past'. So it may seem that the battle for tribal land and language is a peripheral issue, a quaint skirmish at the very edges of relevance. But these voices speak for a vast sector of human history, reaching into aspects, if not the histories, of us all.

It may also seem that tribal demands are anachronistic, appeals against irreversible modernity. That they are disingenuous: most tribal peoples embrace the new, seeing opportunities as well as dangers, taking their place, therefore, as actors and not victims even within the colonial frontiers. But modern tribals are not arguing for a reinstatement of the past. Rather, they seek to have their own resources with which to prosper in the present. With the lands and languages that are indeed theirs, they can live with every kind of opportunity and the strengths of both culture and individual health. This is true for Nunavut, the new Inuit territory within Canada, as it is for the =Khomani deal with South Africa in the southern Kalahari (Page 76). Even at the margins of modern nation states, in the regions that are left to them, they, like everyone, need to live from the centre of themselves. ❏

Hugh Brody *is an anthropologist and film-maker. He has lived with hunter-gatherers in the Arctic and Subarctic, and is now working with the San community of the Southern Kalahari. His books include* The People's Land, Living Arctic *and* Maps and Dreams. *He was a member of the World Bank's Morse Commission in western India*

GEORGE GOSNELL

Memories of school

I was born in Canyon City in 1944, and my parents were in the fishing business. My dad was a fisherman and my mother was a net mender, a net woman it was called in them days; it's still called that today.

In 1952 I had word, they had word, that they were going to send me to Litton Indian Residential School. In 1952. And I only heard then what the residential school was; but I never knew exactly what to expect. It was nice, the train ride that accompanied the getting from Sunnyside Cannery to the town of Litton, which is in the Fraser Valley. I got on the train some time in September. The train ride, at that time, was three days long. It was very, very – how would I say it now? – sort of an adventurous type of trip on the train that time. I really enjoyed the trip.

And we were out in Litton, that was the town of Litton. The residential school was about three and a half, four kilometres from the town of Litton. This was the St George's Residential School.

When we got to Litton, the frightening parts of the trip that are coming in settled in on me. I was already missing my parents. See, that's three days away. And the stay at the residential school in the olden days was one year. You're away from your parents for one year. Your sisters, your brothers, uncles, grandfathers. Very difficult time.

We got off the train at Litton and I didn't know how they were going to transport us from the train station to the residential school. At that time I hardly knew anything about vehicles or a bus. So we all stood there. It must have been about 35, 40 students at the train station at that time. So a few minutes went by. Then there was this truck, there was this dump truck that came around the corner. Everybody looked at each other. It was a dump truck that they used, it's an ordinary dump truck

St Paul's School, Medium Boys – Credit: Anglican Church of Canada, General Synod Archives

where they put us all. We all stood on the back of the dump truck. And remember, this is about 1:30, maybe 2:00, in the morning. It was a very chilly morning, that morning, and we weren't dressed to stand up on the back of a dump truck. That was our transportation from the town of Litton to the Indian residential school known as St George's.

We were all standing in the back of this dump truck, for maybe about 10, 15 minutes – I guess it took about that on the trip to the actual school. We arrived there and there was only about three or four lights that were in front of the school at that time. I don't know how to, how to – I could explain that it sort of felt like you were going to go inside like a prison. That's the frightening feeling come into you.

We were there and we were introduced to the principal at that time. We all walked into the school, the waiting area they called it at that time. I could feel the sadness coming in. I could feel the sadness coming into me, because I knew I was going to be confined in this place for one year. The smell of the school was nothing like I ever smelled before. It was the sort of heavy kind of medicine type of smell in there. And the time now is about 2:00am, maybe 2:30am. And we were advised to follow this one lady up to number one dormitory.

That's where I was put, in number one dormitory. There was about three other kids with me that time. The other students went in number two or number three or number four dormitories. Our dormitory was right on top.

I walked into the dormitory and there was about 40 children lying in nice neat little rows, beds there, maybe 40, maybe 50 students in the dormitory. Dormitory number one. And nobody got up that time, but we were told where our beds were, and I didn't know what to do. I didn't take my clothes off, because there were so many children about there.

I hardly slept that night; maybe not even an hour's sleep. I was too frightened. The next morning, I'd say it was about 7:00, 7:30 maybe – I forgot the exact time – maybe 6:30, and everybody started getting up.

A lady comes through the door and hollered at everybody. Told everybody to get up, wash up and get ready for breakfast. I was in there; I looked around; like I said, there must be 40, 50 children in that dormitory, dormitory number one.

The first thing I noticed right away was how they looked. They had a very strange look in their faces. Their hair was completely cut right off. They had very short hair cuts and their eyes didn't look – they didn't look very happy at all – very sad-looking eyes. Very frightening thing to see. First time I've ever seen anything like that in my life.

And then we went down to what they call the dining room after we washed up. Again, this is a very, very strange place. I've never been in a dining room before where there was so many children. It had big long tables. It must be 20 to 30 students there in one table. And it had one guy that's on the end that passes the food. He is the guy that looks after the table.

How the food came in is in big, big buckets, maybe big pots, that was passed on to that older guy that sat on the end. He was the one who served the breakfast at that time. It was mostly – what do you call it? – oats, or mush, or whatever you call it. Small little bowl, two slices of bread and one glass of milk, and that was our breakfast. It didn't take me long that morning, I got really hungry. I'd got used to eating all the time. You can't do that in the residential school. You only eat at a certain time.

So after that, after the breakfast, we went out. The main school was here, and where we had our classroom was a little bit outside, about 50 feet away from the main school. We were introduced. We were known as the northern group of native children that was there. The people that came from the southern part were called the southern group. So this is how it went all the way, all the way through the year, we were known as the northerners.

And I didn't know how to speak English at that time. I knew very little English language. And I tried to use our own Nisga'a language. That's when I found out the harsh realities of being confined in a residential school. I didn't expect to get strapped that time, but I did. I went to the principal's office and I got strapped for using our own language. Strapped once on each hand. The second time they catch you speaking your language, you are strapped twice on each hand.

All through the year I was caught using my language four times. So the strap was very big, something like a leather belt, very wide and heavy. And when the principal strapped you he didn't do it in a gentle way. He did it in a very harsh way. He talked to you very sternly. Pushed you around. 'You are not supposed to use your language in this school,' was his words. 'You did not come here to learn your own language, the native language. You are now here, inside these school walls, to learn education as we see it,' is how he said it.

And my heart was beating very fast at that time. I didn't understand what the meaning of his words were. But a few minutes passed after I got strapped. I didn't want to go back to the classroom. I sat in the hallway until after dinner. I sat there for about two hours. After I got strapped I didn't want to back to the classroom. I didn't want anybody to see me cry. Sometimes they'd send you into this little room where, I guess, you could go and cry. Very quiet little room, small little room where they sent me, and I don't know if they took the other students there. I would imagine they did.

That's when you get strapped by a strange person in strange

surroundings. It's very difficult to try and grasp what they really wanted you to do. I remember my parents. I wasn't the only one that got the strap. There was quite a few children, both northern group and southern group, got the strap for using their own language.

I don't know why the residential school. I don't know why they had such far distant places for education. To get torn apart from your parents and your brothers and your sisters to educate us.

They educated us all right. They made us forget our own language. God gave us our own language. It was taken away. They were trying to take our language away.

We have a very colourful past. But the language is very important to express yourself, to be able to talk about your grandparents, the chiefs, the important things that have happened in the past. The Nisga'a language is very important to talk about – you cannot really use the English language because meanings disappear in the English language. Not like when we use our own Nisga'a language: meanings come out crystal clear when you are speaking.

Christmas was a very hard time for the residential school students, especially the northern students, because the southern students were allowed to go home. But we had to stay in the school during the Christmas holiday. Very sad time, Christmas time, in the residential school.

And then in the summer, after the school was finally finished with our one year, our time in the residential school was over, we came back on the train. Again the trip took three days. I got off the train. I looked in my mother's face. And I used English.

She asked me why I used the English. I told her that's what we went away for.

I forgot the Nisga'a language that time. It took me many years to use it. Through the help of my father and my mother, I relearned the Nisga'a language.

See, we were brought up in the residential school to use the English language, and they said you cannot use your own Nisga's language. And when we finally got back home, my mom in the Nass valley, when we were using the English language, said: 'That's not your own language.' They said: 'Use your own language.'

I could only count in Nisga'a to 20, but my daughter, she comes home [from the new Nisga'a school in Aiyansh] and she speaks to me in Nisga'a and she can go way past my little 20. ❑

George Gosnell is a Nisga'a Indian, living in the village of Aiyansh in the Nass river valley. The above is excerpted from his interview for 'Time Immemorial', from the TV documentary series As long as the rivers run *(Tamarack Productions)*

JOHN MILLOY

When a language dies

For over a century, the Canadian government suppressed the language and learning of its aboriginal peoples through a system of enforced schooling in 'civilised' culture. The system was only abandoned in 1986; the pain it inflicted, as well as the problems it created, live on

In the early 1990s, the Commissioners of the Federal Royal Commission on Aboriginal Peoples, set up in 1992 in the wake of the Mohawk occupation at Oka, crossed the country holding public hearings. Many people, leaders of aboriginal organisations but ordinary men and women too, stepped forward – witnesses to the too often depressed conditions of their communities and to the scarred lives of friends, family members and neighbours. They spoke of a history of government wardship, economic marginalisation and aggressive Christian missionisation, forces that had integrated them into Canadian society but only as an impoverished minority in their own land. 'It is,' Chief Eli Mandamin told the commissioners, 'the damage inflicted on our First Nations cultures by everything from epidemics to boarding schools to systematic legal discrimination against our cultures that brought our Aboriginal people to the point where it has been difficult to survive.'

The witnesses spoke their pain and notably, though Canada is officially bilingual in French and English, they spoke, almost without exception, in the English language. The majority of aboriginal people in Canada can speak no other tongue and when they come together in regional and national organisations (indeed, when appearing before the commission) its use is a necessity for it is their only common means of communication. At contact there were some 50 indigenous languages. Some have disappeared entirely; others are at the point of extinction.

Credit: Manitoba Museum of Man and Nature

There is in that, and aboriginal people know it, a profound and pervasive tragedy. Alex Denny, Grand Captain of the Micmac Grand Council, gave some sense of that when he spoke of the dying off of the old language speakers. 'We have lost a hell of a lot. Every time an elder dies, commission members, we lose more than a generation, more than several generations of understanding, of comprehending. After 500 years the only thing we can say is we have survived.'

These languages and the cultures (the 'understanding' and 'comprehending') they conveyed from one generation to the next in sound, symbol, ritual and ceremony died for a number of reasons – in part because of the simple fact of European presence and the flowering of western culture in North America. In the beginning, extensive depopulation, triggered by imported European diseases, disrupted and in some cases killed off whole language groups; currently the lives and languages of aboriginal youth continue to be shaped by the pervasive popular culture of television and radio that reaches into even the most remote communities. But equally critical in the demise of traditional languages has been more overt western activity. In Canada, as another Micmac Captain, John Joe Sark, asserted before the Commission, there has been a persistent government 'policy of destroying our language and culture'. Some 5,000 miles to the west, a Coastal Nuu, Chah-Nulth Councillor, Charlie Cootes, termed those same policies a joint church-government 'attempt to wipe out our heritage, our very existence as a distinct people. In a word, they attempted genocide'.

Such policies, persisted in by the government for over a century, are now recognised as having brought aboriginal communities from independent self-sufficiency to a sorrowful state of dependence and dysfunction. In recognition of which, the Canadian government apologised in 1997: 'Sadly, our history with respect to the treatment of Aboriginal people is not something in which we can take pride. Attitudes of racial and cultural superiority led to the suppression of Aboriginal culture and values ... We must acknowledge that the result of these actions was the erosion of the political, economic and social systems of Aboriginal people and nations.' No policy was more central in that process than residential school education. In its 'abusive campaign for the elimination of languages and identity' and in its attempt to resocialise the children, 'to turn our children ... [into] ... imitation non-Indians, imitation white people', it sapped the bodies and beings of the

children and 'did much', Phil Fontaine, the Grand Chief of the Assembly of Manitoba Chiefs, told the Commission, to 'undermine the integrity of our people'.

Policies of cultural genocide were an integral part of the creation of the Canadian federal state after 1867. Aboriginal people had to be moved out of the way to allow access to the resources that constituted the lifeblood of a modernising state. But in a state organised on Christian, liberal democratic principles, imbued with the dominant evangelical-humanitarian sentiments of the British empire, they could not be abandoned nor, in the interest of public safety, could they be ignored. The nation had a duty – 'a sacred trust with which Providence has invested the country in the charge of and care for the aborigines committed to it' – a duty to 'elevate the Indian from his condition of savagery' and to make 'him a self-supporting member of the State, and eventually a citizen in good standing.' To that end, aboriginal people would face 'the unrelenting weight of the government ... to assimilate', to abandon their culture and to take on that of the immigrant communities surrounding them. In 1920, Duncan Campbell Scott, the long-serving deputy superintendent general of Indian Affairs in the first half of the twentieth century, gave a sense of the government's determination when addressing a parliamentary committee: 'Our objective is to continue until there is not a single Indian in Canada that has not been absorbed into the body politic, and there is no Indian problem and no Indian Department.'

The federal assault on aboriginal culture, which was the prerequisite for the pacification of tribal nations and the eventual assimilation of aboriginal individuals, began with the passage of the first Indian Act in 1869. It gave the Indian Department control entirely of Indian governments and communities, stripping them of any formal, institutional means of participating in their own development and defending their culture. By legislative fiat, Indians became wards of the government. Subsequent legislation, in place until 1951, proscribed important religious rituals – the Sun Dance, sweat lodges and the *potlatch* – that underpinned traditional networks of social and economic relations. Such laws were supplemented by the activities of surveillance agencies: courts, police, medical facilities and what one witness termed 'the injudicious zealousness of child welfare agencies', which together were to ensure that communities and individuals conformed to non-aboriginal standards and norms.

An educational strategy was adopted officially in 1879. Thereafter, residential schools were opened across the country to be co-managed by the Department of Indian Affairs and the major churches (Catholic, Anglican, Presbyterian and United). By 1931, the high point of the system, there were 80 in operation and the system grew again in the 1950s as part of the nation's expansion into Inuit homelands. Thousands of children each year, in some years as many as 11,000, were taken into the schools. Recruitment was facilitated by coercive measures. Compulsory education legislation was passed and Indian agents were empowered to enforce the law through their control of family-allowance payments – an income supplement that was critical for families who could normally find only seasonal employment. It was not until 1986 that the system came to an end.

The rationale for the schools was simple and, as it turned out, deadly. Children from the age of six to 16 were to be removed from their communities, from their parents, 'the old unimprovable people', and thus from the baleful, savage 'influence of the wigwam'. They were then to be 'kept constantly within the circle of civilised conditions', the residential schools, where, receiving the 'care of a mother', the children would undergo 'the transformation from the natural condition to that of civilisation', a resocialising process by a movement from circle to square: from a world to be navigated by belief, dreams and spirit guidance to one of secular logic and reasoning; from learning by living, observing and doing, to living and learning by discipline in preparation for a life governed by the dictates of an alien society. Such a metamorphosis and skill training – trades and agriculture for boys, domestic crafts for girls – would enable them to find places in 'white' Canada or to return to their communities to create for all a civilised future.

Even in thought, before the residential concept took the form of badly built, unsafe and unhealthy structures providing not maternal care but too often inadequate food and clothing and a third-class education, there was a dark contradiction, a 'savagery', in the mechanics of civilising the children. The rhetoric itself revealed what would have to be the essentially violent nature of the school system in its assault on child and culture. 'The education that took place in those residential schools,' Emile Bell told the commission, 'was an assault on my people, our people, in the areas of language and identity.' That 'assault', aimed at severing the inter-generational artery of culture that was the profound connection between parent and child sustaining family and community, was the essence of the 'transformation ... to ... civilisation'. Teachers and staff were directed to employ 'every effort ... against anything calculated to keep fresh in the memories of the children habits and associations which it is one of the main objects of industrial education to obliterate'. By 'persistent tuition' it would be possible to 'kill the Indian in him [the student] and save the man.'

None of the foregoing would be achieved, however, unless the students were first released from the shackles that tied them to their parents, communities and culture. And that, in turn, would not be accomplished, the churches and department realised, simply by separating the children from their parents and bringing them within the 'circle of civilised conditions'. Rather, it required a concerted attack on the ontology, on the basic cultural patterning of the children, on their world view and, therefore, on their language.

That the department and churches understood their main challenge was aboriginal ontology is seen in their identification of language as the most critical issue in the curriculum. It was through language that the child received its cultural heritage; it was the vital connection which had to be cut if progress was to be made. The principal of the Shingwauk school informed the department: 'We make a great point on insisting on the boys talking English, as, for their advancement in civilisation, this is, of all things, the most necessary.' Aboriginal languages could not carry the burden of civilisation, the department believed; they could not 'impart ideas which being entirely outside the experience and environment of the pupils and their parents, have no equivalent expression in their native tongue'. Those ideas were the core concepts of European culture: its own ontology, theology and values. Without them, without the English language, the department declared in its Annual Report of 1895, the aboriginal person is 'permanently disabled'. He and his community are beyond the pale of assimilation and not fully amenable to state regulation. 'So long as he keeps his native tongue, so long will he remain a community apart.'

School principals were left to determine how to implement the language policy. Some instituted imaginative systems of positive reinforcement through rewards, prizes or privileges for the exclusive use of English. More often than not, however, the common method was punishment and thus along with general neglect, physical and sexual abuse, what might be termed language abuse joined a sorrowful catalogue of mistreatment with profound consequences for children and thereafter for their communities. There are many sources that detail the mistreatment of children, and over 2,000 court cases, most of which are based on statements of claims for abuse. An Inuit woman's testimony stands eloquently for the experience of thousands:

'After a lifetime of beatings, going hungry, standing in a corner on one leg, and walking in the snow with no shoes for speaking Inuvialuktun, and having a stinging paste rubbed on my face, which they did to stop us from expressing our Eskimo custom of raising our eyebrows for yes and wrinkling our noses for no, I soon lost the ability to speak my mother tongue. When a language dies, the world dies, the world it was generated from breaks down too.'

That language loss destroyed the child's aboriginal world did not mean that the children were transformed, were brought simultaneously to civilisation. Rather, the event of separation from parents and from culture proved to be traumatic and severely debilitating. Anecdotal comments in Indian Department files gave evidence that often the socialisation did not take; that, for example, the schools did not inculcate in the children the key prerequisites for assimilation: 'individual acting and thinking', 'individuality and self-control'. Some agents identified even darker results. One reported 'far too many girls ... turning out prostitutes and boys becoming drunken loafers'. Another opposed the schools because, in his estimation, a great number of ex-students were 'useless' when they returned to their communities. It would have been, he concluded, 'far better that they never go to school than turn out as the ex-pupils have done'.

In the decade and a half since the system was closed, aboriginal people have not been silent on that struggle, on the consequences of the schools. They have spoken of what is popularly known as the 'residential school syndrome' – a complex social pathology of deviant behaviour with a corrosive and persistent trans-'generational impact' that, as one witness before the commission observed, 'just eats its way like a cancer, to me, my nephews, my nieces and it will continue'. Consultants working for the Assembly of First Nations detailed some of the pathologies that constitute the 'syndrome':

'The survivors of the Indian residential schools have, in many cases, continued to have their lives shaped by the experiences in these schools, continue to struggle with their identity after years of being taught to hate themselves and their culture. The residential schools led to a disruption in the transference of parenting skills from one generation to the next. Without those skills, many survivors had had difficulty in raising their own children. In residential schools, they learned that adults often exert power through abuse. The lessons learned in childhood are often repeated in adulthood with the result that many survivors of the residential school system often inflict abuse on their own children. These children in turn use the same tools on their children.'

Witnesses before the commission were certainly less circumspect about the 'lessons learned' and the abuse inflicted across generations. During his testimony, Phil Fontaine, National Chief of the Assembly of First Nations, noted that the consequences of the schools are yet 'all around us in our communities, in our urban centres, wherever you have First Nation people, aboriginal people. That experience spills over and translates into domestic violence, violence against women, against children, sexual abuse'. Other witnesses added the details: 'So many fell victim to violence, accidents, addictions and suicide', living with 'the same legacy of broken families, broken culture and broken spirit'. The 'brutality of it killed our spirits' and thus the 'road to suicide was being paved'. We 'learned that the way to discipline a child is with violence and raised voices, not love and caring', so that many of those 'young people are suffering out on the streets' today. 'Many of our Elders,' who were students in the past, 'believe that our culture is inferior ... they continue to carry around the pain they suffered there ... they pass it on to the youth like us', for 'they are unable to live independently of the non-aboriginal structures or policies instilled within them', and, therefore, 'they have normalised the destruction of their culture, tradition, lands and resources. They have become a nation of people who have normalised their own oppression.' And the sadness of the witnesses was palpable: 'The hurt is still there whenever residential schools are brought up. It brings back memories, it brings back tears. Even as old men we cry. We cry when we remember those years.'

Persistently, amid those memories witnesses returned to the critical issues of language and culture. 'I think we would all agree,' the Micmac Elder Albert Marshall asserted, 'that residential schools have contributed the most in the loss of our tradition, our culture, and the very sense of

living and losing our spirituality.' The equation, Emile Trip-De-Roche
explained to the commissioners, is really very simple: 'Anywhere they
placed a residential school, the local people usually lost their language.
Anywhere there is no residential school, the people have retained the
language which is so important to them.' Unfortunately, communities
that escaped contact with the schools were few and far between.

The imposition of English in the schools isolated individuals from
their culture and destroyed the balance of communities; it produced
'personal, family and community dysfunctions'. 'Words are more potent
than a gun, I think,' said another witness, Herb Nabigon. 'If we
remember, in residential schools the words that were thrown at us and
the damage is still with us today.' Indeed, the words, ex-students testified,
often focused on language use. They were taught that 'to speak Indian
was no good. Of course, if you have that pounded into you when you
are a child, you are going to believe that.' And thus many people 'walked
away from those institutions with a lot of personal problems'. 'We have a
high rate of alcoholism, suicide rate, family break-ups. A lot of our
young people are on drugs or on booze.'

Those problems would not easily be resolved for the many individuals
who returned home from school 'unable to speak our language' and
without any knowledge of 'the cultural traditions, the government
system, the oral histories and the stories and the legends'. Having lost
culture and language, they also lost 'many of the values of life' and thus
were unable 'to fit in any more with their people'. On returning home,
they had, in a sense, entered a foreign land, 'they couldn't speak to their
parents any more or their community'. And there was no way home
through the English language, no way back to ceremonies that
confirmed the individual's place in the community and guided life along
positive channels: no way 'because the English language, which most of
us speak, does not adequately capture the spirit of our teachings'. And
for many, home itself was not even an attractive destination. 'Indian' had
become an unacceptable identity. Here again language was a factor.
'Having had the language beaten out of them in one way or another
they have shame of their own language or not a complete pride for their
own language.' Some traditional language speakers 'were really
frightened of even talking to their children openly about our spiritual
development and others would not teach the language to children
'because they didn't want their children to experience the same

treatment' in the schools.

In commission sessions, the witnesses spoke of their pain but they spoke, too, of their hopes for 'cultural resurgence' and of their belief in 'a better life tomorrow again'. They may be a minority in their own land but they are also, Chief Norman Stinson assured the commission, 'survivors in our own land'. And despite the social and psychological crisis that envelops many communities, 'we can change that victim identity to a survivor identity'.

There are, today, movements across the face of aboriginal Canada determined to do that: 'to seek out and reclaim their own history' and, most important, 'to catch back up on our language'. Catching back up, based on yet scarce human resources – the Elders who still speak – is taking place in community-based adult education programmes, in the classrooms of community-controlled schools and in university courses using digital technology to teach, research and restore the language. Coming back, too, are the ceremonies: the Elders' conferences, the sweats, the drum groups and pow-wows, the traditions and teachings. And, in the light of that knowledge, people are redesigning community-based institutions that were, in the past, the instruments of colonial manipulation – schools, land government, health-care facilities and justice forums. 'We can change our lives and our communities so as to restore our dignity and self-respect,' Pat Shore, president of the National Native Association of Treatment Directors, assured the commission. The path back to dignity that communities have charted is a return to language and to culturally appropriate institutions of self-determination.

The future will not, however, see the banishment of English. It will remain the only language for many and the other language, perhaps, for a growing number who also have fluency in a traditional tongue. It will still be needed to speak to other Canadians and to speak across tribal boundaries. But it might not be the same English or, at least, might not function solely as the colonising force that it has been in the past. To hear English spoken in many communities is to hear an indigenised language. And the growing number of aboriginal authors, playwrights, songwriters and poets who are using English – Thomson Highway, Buffy Sainte-Marie, Leonore Keeshig-Tobias, Thomas King and Beth Brant for instance – are using it as their own. Through it, for example, they have called upon the trickster of traditional narratives (Old Man, Coyote etc) and positive hybrid icons of the post-contact period (the

Indian-cowboy) to emphasise ways in which Indianess was and remains so much more than the restrictive stereotypes of the eighteenth and nineteenth centuries, and to subvert old categories, ('savage' and 'civilised)' that were the text and pretext of Canadian dominance and of the self-proclaimed cultural superiority upon which rested the residential school system and those other policies of cultural genocide. ❏

John Milloy is an historian at Peter Robinson College, Trent University, Ontario

LESLIE HALL PINDER

The carriers of no

When the landclaims of aboriginal people came to court in Canada, the judge was embarrased and a whole culture found itself on trial

April 1991. I have been thinking about different kinds of announcements.

If someone tells me, 'I have bad news,' I prepare myself for the kind of thing I have heard before. I know what it might be; I start to imagine what has happened.

Or if someone says, 'I have good news,' a different body set: expectant, open, being ready.

But if someone says, 'I have strange news to tell you', that's different.

I have an urgent desire to tell you something and at the same time I am thinking about embarrassment and strangeness and not really understanding what has happened.

After four years in the courts, Chief Justice Allan McEachern of the Supreme Court of British Columbia, Canada, had completed his reasons for judgment in the Gitksan-Wet'suwet'en land claims litigation. The case was about many things, but mainly whether or not Britain, and later Canada, had the legal obligation to enter into treaties with the aboriginal people. Because over most of British Columbia there are no treaties, no compacts or arrangements. The settlers simply moved in and have stayed. The title of the Crown has not been quieted. This case was about whether underneath the Crown's claim to title there was a more basic 'original' title which was a contender.

At the direction of the Chief Justice, all the lawyers who had worked on the case were told to meet at the courthouse at 7am, 8 March 1991, in Vancouver. We would be sequestered for two hours with the decision and then set free to announce our respective interpretations of the case and its consequences.

Two hours later, we were led back out of that room, through the judge's entrance into a courtroom and out into the Great Hall. I saw one of my clients, a Secwepemc woman, standing across that vast space. She started to come towards me, smiling. She had a wide smile as she moved toward me almost floating. And my movements became weightless and slow as I shook my head no and faster as I put my hands up and said, 'No,' pushing so she would go back. It seemed there was a sniper on the roof and she didn't know that he was there. I had seen him. I had seen him on the inside; he had climbed the stairs to the top of the building, he was on the roof and he had a gun. I pushed her back so that she would get down, lie low. 'There's a sniper.' And she slowly stopped coming towards me and turned, confused, as she started to move away. 'It's a brutal judgment,' I said. 'Hide. It's all over. Protect yourself.'

The decision is a devastation. The judge ruled that the rights of the Gitksan-Wet'suwet'en who live in the northern interior of the province – and indeed the rights of all aboriginal people in BC – had been extinguished by the colonial government simply intending to bring settlers into their territory. Nothing more was required: no treaties, no compensation, no deals. The natives had no claims.

The judge said it wasn't the Indians' land being taken from them which destroyed their sense of identity, nor did the introduction of alcohol, epidemics and limited economic opportunities result from settlers taking their land. Strangely, he held that the land was seldom able to provide the Indians with anything more than a primitive existence. However, he concluded that 'there is much wood left in the territory'; the Indians should still be able to sustain themselves. After land has been clear-cut logged, it becomes 'usable again' and the aboriginal people may then re-enter the land 'for subsistence purposes until such time as it is dedicated [by the Crown] to another purpose'.

But it is not even the result of the decision which makes it so devastating. There have been major defeats before, as well as victories. It is the contents of the reasoning, it is what the judge says about knowledge, about information, about who we are as a society which has stunned me.

In what I say I mean no disrespect to Judge McEachern. He is now the Chief Justice of the BC Court of Appeal. In what he says and believes, he represents the best of what we have to offer.

The case is referred to as the Gitksan-Wet'suwet'en case because of the two Indian nations represented. The case bears the name of one of the house chiefs, Delgamuukw. The high chief who carried the name Delgamuukw died before judgment. Now his brother has been passed the name.

Judge McEachern was embarrassed throughout the trial and he told us that. The first time he mentioned it was when the lawyers for the Gitksan-Wet'suwet'en asked that the case be heard mostly in the small village of Smithers, BC, instead of miles away in Vancouver, because that was closest to the Indian people's territory. He would be there; the natives could readily come to the court.

The judge said that he was judicially embarrassed by the request.

I started listening to that word and when people used it. He was embarrassed by the length of the trial. He was embarrassed at the evidence that was called.

He was embarrassed when Mary Johnson, one of the Elders, wanted to sing her song to him in court during the telling of her *adaawk*.

The *adaawk* is the oral history which carries the people's stories, their relationship to their territory, their spirit songs. It is the *adaawk* that the people wanted to tell the judge. It is their evidence, their proof, their case. It answered everything that the lawyers for the province put forward. To embarrass means to make difficult by obstructions. Encumbered. To be impeded.

Mary Johnson was telling the judge her *adaawk*. She said: 'A brother and two sisters were travelling. The brother, Wildim Waax, starved to death because they couldn't find anything to eat. And not long after he died, they heard the drumming grouse, and the elder sister lay down near the log where the grouse drums. Whenever a grouse is drumming, he always comes back to the same spot where he drums, an old log covered with moss, and it's soft. So the elder sister hid herself underneath the moss beside the log, but she missed the grouse. Then the young sister lay down. She caught the grouse and they killed the grouse, so they sat down and they both cried. They remember their brother that's just died and they compose a dirge song.'

And Peter Grant, the lawyer, says: 'In telling of this *adaawk*, is this the place where you would sing the dirge song? Mary Johnson says: 'Yes.' The lawyer says: 'Go ahead, you can sing the song.'

And the judge says: 'Is the wording of the song necessary?'

The lawyer says: 'Yes.'

And the judge says: 'I don't want to be sceptical, but I have some difficulty in understanding why the actual wording of the song is necessary.'

The witness says: 'Do you want me to sing the song?'

The lawyer says: 'Yes.'

And the judge says: 'Are you going to ask the witness to now sing the song?'

The lawyer says: 'The song is part of the history, and I am asking the witness to sing the song as part of the history, because the song itself invokes the history.'

The judge says: 'How long is it?'

The lawyer says: 'It's not very long. It's very short.'

The judge says : 'Could it not be written out and the witness asked if this is the wording? We are on the verge of getting way off track here. To have witnesses singing songs in court is not the proper way to approach this problem... I just say, with respect, I've never heard it happen before, I never thought it was necessary, and I don't think it necessary now. It doesn't seem to me she has to sing it.'

And the lawyer says: 'It's a song which itself invokes the history and the depth of the history of what she is telling. It is necessary for you to appreciate –'

The judge says: 'I have a tin ear, Mr Grant. It's not going to do any good to sing to me.'

Mr Grant says: 'I would ask, Mrs Johnson, if you could go ahead and sing the song.'

And the witness says: 'It's a sad song when they raise the pole, and when the pole is halfway up, they told the chiefs that pull the rope to stop for a few minutes, and they sang the song and they cried. If the court wants me to sing it, I'll sing it.'

And the judge says: 'No I don't, Mrs Johnson. I don't think that this is the way this part of this trial should be conducted. I just don't think it's necessary. I think it is not the right way to present the case.'

The lawyer says: 'You can go ahead and sing the song now.'

And Mary Johnson sings her song. She sings about the grouse flying. How the grouse gave himself up to die for the sisters to help them save their lives. 'And today the young lady that caught the grouse stood at the foot of our totempole that we restored in 1973 and she is holding the grouse with tears in her eyes.'

And when Mary Johnson has finished, the judge says: 'All right, Mr Grant, would you explain to me, because this may happen again, why you think it was necessary to sing the song? This is a trial, not a performance.'

Mr Grant says that the Gitksan-Wet'suwet'en expressed their ownership of their territory through their regalia, their *adaawk*, and their songs.

The judge says: 'I don't find that a persuasive argument at all. It is not necessary in a matter of this kind for that song to have been sung, and I think that I must say now that I ought not to have been exposed to it. I don't think it should happen again. I think I'm being imposed upon and I don't think that should happen in a trial like this. I see no reason whatsoever why it was necessary to ask her to sing that song. Go on with the evidence, please.'

In a trial the word 'embarrassed' describes what it feels like when you are presented with the unacceptable. It is the visceral effects of the disallowed, of something that does not fit our idea of information, knowledge, fact. It is the body's discomfort at being at the edge of a path.

The judge was embarrassed by the *adaawk*.

His judgment upholds the idea that everyone in western society sees things objectively; and everyone who belongs to an aboriginal society see things in a subjective, romantic, biased way.

The judge had 'serious doubts about the reliability of the *adaawk* as evidence'. Oral traditions are not reliable. 'Even when employed carefully, memory ethnography can only provide totally accurate information for relatively short time spans, usually 100 years at the very most.' Therefore oral history can only 'fill in the gaps' left at the 'end of a purely scientific investigation'. Further, 'I am able to make the required findings about the history of these people' without the evidence of the anthropologist. There were also flaws in the archeological evidence because 'any aboriginal people could have created these remains'.

The plaintiffs' evidence was discounted, reduced, diminished, sometimes even in a kindly way, 'reluctantly, without intending any affront to the beliefs of these peoples'.

But the evidence of a life-long nonIndian resident of the territory was taken as truth. He hadn't heard the Indians say they claimed ownership of the territory. He hadn't noticed many of them on the land.

The judge also accepted the documentary evidence of the journal kept by the white trader at the Hudson's Bay Company. He is 'one of our most useful historians', who had a Fort on Babine Lake in 1822 and described the 'primitive condition of the natives'. That condition was 'not impressive'.

'Many of the badges of civilisation, as we of European culture understand that term, were indeed absent. The plaintiffs' ancestors had no written language, no horses or wheeled vehicles, slavery and starvation were not uncommon, wars with neighbouring peoples were common, and there is no doubt that aboriginal life in the territory was, at best, nasty, brutish and short'

The Gitksan-Wet'suwet'en people, with their extraordinary art, the vast and visible manifestations of their culture, are described as having a 'low level of civilisation'.

In the face of others' disbelief, in the face of others discounting them, not accepting what they have to say, some aboriginal people go into themselves with their information and their knowledge. They withdraw; they take back their stories. They move to higher ground. They don't tell their stories. They are careful who receives the wisdom.

An Elder from Bella Coola told me she would rather have her stories die than tell them to someone who wasn't ready to hear.

With this court case, the rights of the aboriginal people have been extinguished.

And there is this pervasive idea of emptiness. How often the judge refers to it. 'The most striking thing that one notices in the territory away from the Skeena-Bulkley corridor is its emptiness ... The territory is, indeed, a vast emptiness.'

But that country is inhabited by Innu.

The judge says: 'If the land is substantially empty now ... then I believe it was also empty for aboriginal purposes at the time of contact.' Their rights over empty territory are easily, bloodlessly, put out.

After the judgment I am thrown back. I go to the library. I buy books. I yearn for something that is part of my cultural traditions which will answer the world view in this judgment. I am searching for some wisdom which will not leave me feeling so bereft. I am still looking. I bring my search here.

I find a book by Henry Nash Smith about the symbolism of the American West. A reviewer says that the book is devoid of Indians because 'the author took as the dominant view of the frontier the classic concept of it as a vast emptiness awaiting peaceful occupation by agrarian pioneers'.

Other books show the image of our frontier hero: a man revered for his ability to deal with a savage environment but not succumb to such savagery, not to forget that one is the agent for one's own culture, representing order and progress. I find Slotkin saying American history is viewed as a 'heroic scale Indian war, pitting race against race', and the central concern of the mythmakers is with the problem of reaching the 'end of the frontier' the place of the 'last stand'.

The frontier of violence is between civilised whites and red savages. It is a myth peculiar to our culture.

Who is it that defends civilisation against such chaos in the perpetual war between civilisation and savagery?

In the books, the noble pathfinders who view nature as the source of all wisdom are doomed, just as the natives are doomed. Such people have to face extinction before the march of civilisation because they were incapable or unwilling to adapt.

The judge says: 'It is obvious [the Indians] must make their way off the reserves. The difficulties of adapting to changing circumstances, not limited land use, is the principal cause of Indian misfortune.'

Now, in court, the combat-lawyers for the government sneer. In a new case they refer to the limited reserve land which the Indians have as 'free land the Indians got'. They unveil their contempt.

Then I am embarrassed. I am ashamed.

This judgment is the judicial equivalent of a nuclear winter. The face of civilisation is barbaric.

After clear-cut logging leaves the land wasted and barren, it may be re-used by the Indians for sustenance.

What counts as information or fact? What can sustain us?

With more and more sophisticated technology we have destroyed the stories. In court cases, we word-search transcripts to reassemble the evidence; it doesn't resemble anything that was said by anyone. We cut the words, even our written words, away from the context, and hold them up as pieces of meaning, hacked-up pieces of meaning.

As lawyers we don't have to take any responsibility for constructing a world. We only have to destroy another's construction. We say no. We are the civilised, well-heeled, comfortable carriers of no. We thrive on it.

Other races die.

'I flew over the territory. I was struck by its emptiness.'

This judgment has humiliated the people. I hear the Indian leaders say to one another, 'We must tell the children they are as good as anybody, that we aren't just dogs.'

As though it is not enough to defeat the enemy; they have to be degraded and humiliated too.

I have an old map from the 1860s and on it there is a place with an Indian name that is shown as a reserve. The Elders know about it; they say the word; they give its meaning. The reserve is not on any of the new maps.

I call the library. I ask the man in the reference section if he can find any record of this place.

The librarian goes away.

I wait.

I think of him as a fisherman. Sometimes he uses a net but now he is being asked to dive.

He is gone a long time. I wait. I keep looking at this map.

He is fishing with his hands for a name in the past that some one of us, from our culture, has written down.

I am waiting on the telephone. The librarian has been gone a long time, looking for what was written down. And I wait, hoping for information, for knowledge. Hoping that at one time someone wrote down a word in another's language, a place-name that carried a story, and that we put it on a map. The story will still exist, even if it wasn't written down. But it will go further away, to higher ground, and we will be the losers.

Go right up to the edge of embarrassment, take yourself there, go over the edge. Information comes as a bird hitting the window, or as a fish hitting a net. Go fishing. I urge you to go fishing.

April 1999. On 25 June 1993, the lawyers were once again sequestered to receive judgment from the Court of Appeal. The court was deeply divided. Three judges upheld the lower court decision, and two judges found in favour of the Gitksan Wet'suwet'en. All the judges, however, ruled that aboriginal rights were not extinguished. But although they still exist, they are greatly diminished. As long as the native people live as their forefathers had lived – as long as they do not enter the modern world or compete in the 'commercial mainstream' – they have their original rights.

The Gitksan Wet'suwet'en appealed the case to the Supreme Court of Canada. Before the case was heard they spent a number of years trying to negotiate a settlement with the Crown, but without success. Finally, the case was argued; seven judges of the highest court in Canada gave their decision on 11 December 1998.

The judges said that although a total of 61 witnesses gave evidence at trial – the longest trial in western judicial history – and:

'... 53 territorial affidavits were filed; 30 deponents were cross-examined out of court; there are 23,503 pages of transcript evidence at trial; 5,898 pages of transcript of argument; 3,039 pages of commission evidence and 2,553 pages of cross-examination on affidavits ... about 9,200 exhibits were filed at trial comprising ... well over 50,000 pages; the plaintiffs' draft outline of argument comprises 3,250 pages, the province's 1,975 pages, and Canada's over 1,000 pages; there are 5,977 pages of transcript of argument in hard copy and on diskettes ... The result was a judgment of over 400 pages in length ...'

Nevertheless, a new trial had to be ordered. This was because Judge McEachern gave no independent weight at all to the oral histories of the native people. Judge McEachern was wrong to have discounted these histories, believing they were only romantic versions of the truth, that they were not 'literally true'.

By having a 'tin ear' the judge was unable to hear all that he should have heard. And it was impossible for the appeal judges to correct this.

But this aspect of the ruling, alone, is heartening. The common law has been made to expand some, to allow in different ways of belief and knowing, different ways of telling what is true.

The judges went on to say other things, to try to give guidance on these difficult questions that have perplexed us for seven generations in Canada. They said, just as oral histories are as sound as the written ones, aboriginal title is as real as legal title. The government must negotiate treaties. The Crown is under a 'a moral, if not a legal, duty to' do so.

What has happened to the sniper on top of the wall? Is he still there?

It has been over a year now since the decision. After the first few months, the government said it was studying the decision. Their policies remain unchanged. Then a few months ago it was announced that over $7 million was going to be given to the National Native Organisation so that they could study the decision over the next two years. The sniper in the western world is the bureaucrat, is the politician, is the minister who fails to take heed of this matter, who doesn't care, who is now the carrier of no.

I am still waiting. ❏

Leslie Hall Pinder is a lawyer, poet and novelist based in Vancouver, Canada

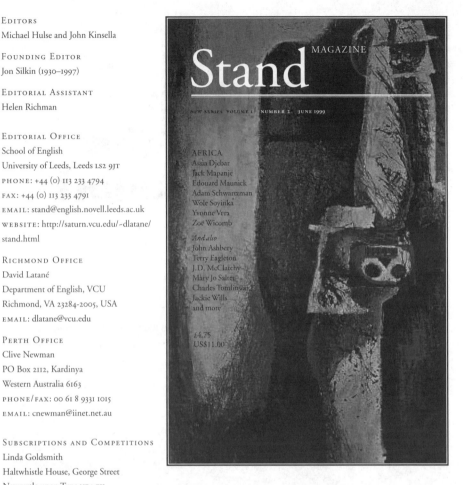

Editors
Michael Hulse and John Kinsella

Founding Editor
Jon Silkin (1930–1997)

Editorial Assistant
Helen Richman

Editorial Office
School of English
University of Leeds, Leeds LS2 9JT
PHONE: +44 (0) 113 233 4794
FAX: +44 (0) 113 233 4791
EMAIL: stand@english.novell.leeds.ac.uk
WEBSITE: http://saturn.vcu.edu/~dlatane/stand.html

Richmond Office
David Latané
Department of English, VCU
Richmond, VA 23284-2005, USA
EMAIL: dlatane@vcu.edu

Perth Office
Clive Newman
PO Box 2112, Kardinya
Western Australia 6163
PHONE/FAX: 00 61 8 9331 1015
EMAIL: cnewman@iinet.net.au

Subscriptions and Competitions
Linda Goldsmith
Haltwhistle House, George Street
Newcastle upon Tyne NE4 7JL
PHONE: +44 (0) 191 273 3280
FAX: +44 (0) 191 272 0040

Subscriptions:
Four issues
£16.00 (UK) £18.00/US$29.00 (overseas)
Unwaged/student:
£10.00 (UK) £12.00/US$22.50 (overseas)
Single copy:
£4.75 (UK) £5.75/US$11.00 (overseas)

Stand'*s Africa issue features: Assia Djebar, Gail Dendy, Edouard Maunick, Adam Schwartzmann, Wole Soyinka, Véronique Tadjo, Zoë Wicomb, Yvonne Vera, prison memoirs of Jack Mapanje, essays on Antjie Krog and Soyinka.*
And also: John Ashbery, Terry Eagleton, J.D. McClatchy, Michael Mott, Mary Jo Salter, Charles Tomlinson, Jackie Wills and much more.

Jimo Akolo, *Man Hanging from a Tree* (oil on canvas, 121 x 182 cm). With thanks to Dennis Duerden for permission to reproduce this image from *African Art*, Hamlyn Publishing, 1968.

HUGH BRODY

Resurrection: ‡Khomani of the southern Kalahari

Anna Kassi: *'Yes, life. How does life move? Does it run straight? Or does it run askew? ... If the Boer talks to us, we must talk Afrikaans to him, and shoot the language. Yet it's the nicest language. These children will speak ... That child, shoots out with the language.'*

Andries Oleyn: *'That is why it is I who sit here ... He who seeks the land of his mother and father and grandfather ... where we walked where we wished ... before the farmers came to trap us ... that is why we are fighting over this thing. We fight for our land.'*

Credit: Benny Gool / Trace Image

Credit: Benny Gool / Trace Image

The dry veldt and deserts of South Africa were the lands of the Bushman, now known as the San. Five hundred years of settlement and colonialism, first by Bantu-speaking immigrants from within Africa and then by heavily armed Europeans, dispossessed and silenced the San. Vast cattle and sheep farms replaced their network of gathering and hunting territories, their camps and communities, their animals and the very environment. Many thousands of San were taken into forced labour, imprisoned (they were the first inmates of Robben Island), hunted down and killed. The farmers' frontier pushed ever further north, across the Karoo, up to the Orange River and, in the twentieth century, to the Kalahari. Brains that understood domestic animals and a rugged low-church Christianity prevailed. An immense encyclopedia of knowledge of those places – of their water, plants, animals, dunes and spirits – was wiped out. Many languages of the San, each carrying the stories and mysteries of their world, disappeared.

Elsie Vaalboi: *'I loved the Bushman language ... If I think about it now, my brothers could all speak Bushman, they all spoke it. But just when the bread came, then it was, "Yes Ma'am, yes."'*

Elsie Vaalboi was born in the early 1900s in the southern Kalahari. She spent most of her adult life as a servant on white farms. Her people, the =Khomani, are the last San society of South Africa, the survivors of the Bushman holocaust. In the 1970s, both the apartheid government and experts on Bushman cultures decreed that the =Khomani had ceased to exist. Linguists announced that the language had died out.
Elsie Vaalboi knew the =Khomani language. But her children didn't, nor did her neighbours. She believed she was the last =Khomani speaker on earth.

Elsie Vaalboi: *'Nothing, nothing. There was nothing, just the bare sand dunes. That's what I don't know – if we scooped up water to drink. We were such naked Bushmen. I just know I ate tsama's and I eat cucumber, and I eat this thing, and that thing. I didn't know about tapwater. Now that I'm so old, now I must find out. In those days, in the Kalahari, we lived without tapwater.'*

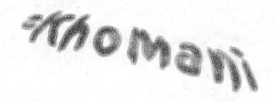

Petrus Vaalboi (holding a weaver bird he has caught with his hands) – Credit: Hugh Brody

Petrus Vaalboi:
'Here I sit, without my mother's language, without my father's language. I am powerless. I only have Afrikaans. I am out. I feel sometimes like an exile. That, that is the sadness. Then you feel how painful it is, if you are without the language. If I could have spoken it ... but I couldn't. I can't. And now, now we have the chance. With the government, to begin to move.'

In 1997, one of Elsie Vaalboi's sons, Petrus, began to work with the South Africa San Institute (SASI), a tiny NGO in Cape Town. They met with =Khomani families who were squatters at Welkom, a community at the edge of the Kalahari Gemsbok National Park, selling crafts and photo opportunities to passing tourists.

Working with Roger Chennells, a human rights lawyer, SASI decided to claim the =Khomani lands. Elsie Vaalboi recorded a message in the =Khomani language, addressed to the Mandela government. Perhaps there was no one in the world who would understand her words, but in Afrikaans she explained: the time had come, she said, for the Bushmen to recover their lands and their lost language. The Boer had to move aside and let the Bushmen live again in their real homes.

SASI began a search for =Khomani survivors. They also looked for speakers of the language. In 1998, they went to Swartkop, a sprawl of shacks and cabins 10 kilometres from Upington, the principal town of the northern Cape. They had heard that there was a =Khomani family living there. They met four women – three sisters and their first cousin. They were thin and frail, in their late sixties and early seventies. They were Bushmen, they said, and they spoke their language. They listened to Elsie's tape. They were amazed and delighted and recorded a message in reply. Yes, they said, they too spoke 'Boesmantal'. And yes, they said, the time had come to fight to get back their lands and to save their language.

Roger Chennells meeting with =Khomani of the Welkom community. credit: *Geoff Perrot/SASI*

Swartkop sisters in the Kalahari Gembsok Park showing where they lived as children – Credit: Ted Chamberlin

SASI took the Swartkop tape to Elsie. She discovered that she was not the only speaker in the world; for the first time in many years she heard her language. She sent a reply. 'If you really do understand my language, then you understand this. We cannot live with the Boer. We must get our land, and live again as ourselves.' The search for the =Khomani diaspora continued. By the beginning of this year, 15 speakers of the language had been found – at the edge of coloured townships, as isolated workers in shacks beside white farms, at the margins. They met, they talked, they shared hopes. And they became the centre of the land claim.

Jakob Malgas and his son in the SASI van, travelling through the Park – Credit: Ted Chamberlin

Family by family, the =Khomani put together the events of the last 50 years. They went into the Kalahari Gembsok Park, where many of them had lived and from where they had been expelled. They went to the places they loved and had known best. They pointed to trees they knew, the graves of their relatives, the best places for each kind of plant. They made lists of =Khomani names for everything. And they set out their grief, and their determination to get back that which was theirs, both land and language.

/Una Rooi: *'I was born here. Here, when I was very young, my grandmother, my father's mother, cut my umbilical cord for me. And there, in the veld, she gathered for me... This is where we lived, where my mother's house stood. I can still see it today, how that place looked. And I become so heartbroken when I look up, out over the branches of the tree ... My tree, my tree, my tree. How could they not have thought that there would be people who would come back, to stand under my tree. My mother buried my cord here. I want so much to take care of my tree.'*

Andries Oleyn: *'There I was born, there I started to become a human being ... Those days I lived just like I could and only on my mother's breast ... Then came the understanding, it started to come. Because when I got my understanding completely, I was already among the farmers, the Boers. Then already the farmers scattered us here and there ... And the farmers, they chased us one by one like sheep ... what were we to do?'*

/Una Rooi: *'They burned out our homes ... Then my father asked him, "Sir, why? Where do you think we must live?" Then he asked my father, "What do you want to do? You are worth nothing, to ask why." Then he kicked my father ... When my father fell, there were four constables and two of them had him by the arms and two by the legs ... Then we ran. And I was always very fond of my brother ... my brother and I ran and said, "Ma." When my father fell, then my mother stood ... and said, "Sir, how can you? That's not a bad word that the man said. He just asked why you were burning our home." And then he said, "Now listen here, meid, on the road." ... They took my father to prison ... And he died, he died. A good man, my father, and killed.'*

Elsie with the Swartkop =Khomani when they visited her at Rietfontein – Credit: Ted Chamberlin

By the beginning of 1999, the =Khomani San demand was taking shape. On the basis of the South African government's land claims legislation, which states that anyone displaced or dispossessed since 1913 by racist laws or procedures can seek restitution or compensation, the =Khomani claimed the Kalahari Gemsbok Park and adjacent lands. After difficult and complex argument, the claim was accepted.

On 21 March 1999, then deputy president Thabo Mbeki, along with minister of land affairs Derek Hanekom, travelled to the southern Kalahari, and met Petrus Vaalboi, Dawid Kruyper, the Swartkop sisters, along with many others. At a formal ceremony they signed an agreement, giving the =Khomani rights to some 50,000 hectares of land within the Kalahari Gemsbok Park and 40,000 hectares outside the park. The details of the agreement are still under negotiation – including the role the =Khomani will play in management of the park, their role in tourism and the creation of a new village site.

Thabo Mbeki: *'We shall mend the broken strings of the distant past so that our dreams can take root. For the stories of the Khoe [Nama] and the San have told us that this dream is too big for one person to hold. It is a dream that must be dreamed collectively, by all the people ... It is by dreaming together – by mending the broken strings that tore us apart in the past – that we shall all of us produce a better life for you who have been the victims of the worst of oppression. It is now my place to say: Here is your land. Take it, look after it and thrive.'*

/Una Rooi: *'/Aise.' 'Thank you.'*

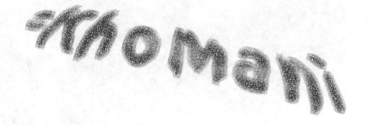

Note: The symbols / and = are used to show the click sound for which San languages are famous

FELIX PADEL

The silence of the forest

As the modern world encroaches on their world, India's 60 million tribals are driven from the forests they have protected for millennia

*A*divasi is the Hindi word most often used in India to refer to tribals, the 'original dwellers' or aboriginals who inhabited the land before the ancestors of the Hindu invaders arrived some 3,000 years ago. Unlike the tribal peoples of North America and Australia, *adivasi* have always been in contact with non-tribals. They lived in forest and mountain regions in between Hindu – and later Muslim – kingdoms, which at different times fought them, ruled them or made treaties with them.

The total population of 'tribals' identified by the Indian administration is about 60 million. It includes peoples whose lives are intertwined with modern India, and others who are utterly remote from mainstream life. The *adivasi* vary a great deal in the degree to which they are Hinduised or 'developed', Christianised or 'modern'.

In most regions, the deciding factor in the effectiveness of those who seek to push one or other version of 'progress' is how well the forest survives, and whether or not the *adivasi* have access to it. An *adivasi* way of life that has resources, rituals, pride and languages that are its own depends on being in and making use of the forest. And in India, the forest has been at extreme risk from successive waves of colonial, economic and administrative domination.

Far from recognising the immense scope and depth of *adivasi* knowledge of the forest, the forest department rarely acknowledges its existence. *Adivasi* ways of speaking of and understanding the forest take a very different form from their own 'scientific' knowledge. The one is based on generations of interdependence; the other on control, profit and distant abstractions. The refusal on the part of Indian forestry officials to hear or see the *adivasi* is deeply embedded, a matter of politics as well as consciousness.

It is a paradox that the forest department, which was set up to protect – but also capitalise on – India's forests, is often the forest's worst exploiter. By limiting tribals' access to the forest and preventing their traditional 'slash and burn' agriculture, which is sustainable in the long term, it contributes to the pressure on tribals to create fields, which destroy the forest permanently. Further, by imposing a web of petty corruption in the form of fines and bribes and court cases, forestry officials have divided *adivasi* from the environment that has always been theirs. The forest, that was their home and theirs to take from, as it was theirs in spirit and worship, is thus turned into the setting for tribal loss, conflict and exploitation.

While *adivasi* are the original occupants and owners of the forests, they are at the bottom of India's hierarchies, below even the lowest in the caste system, and with the least political influence. They are among the poorest of the poor and endure many forms of exploitation. They must bribe officials – especially forest guards – to secure everyday protection; they pay exorbitant rates of interest to moneylenders; they are drawn into the modern world but are least able to negotiate with it.

The exploitation of the *adivasi* is matched by their apparent invisibility and inaudibility. The Indian constitution recognises that the 'Tribes of India' and weakest castes – 'scheduled' castes and tribes – need 'special protection'. This takes the form of measures to guarantee them employment and educational help. But for most tribal groups, especially those deepest in the forests and mountains, these measures and provisions are beyond their reach, if not beyond their awareness. The officials with whom they deal have little respect for scheduled tribes and do nothing to alleviate their vulnerability or give them a voice.

Tribal religion is based on respect for the forest, but the destruction of India's forests since independence is striking: some 50 per cent of the forest that remained in 1948 has been felled for timber or cleared for agriculture. Under pressure from modern economic incursions, even into remote regions, tribals find themselves needing both money and more land. They say that the 'outsiders' have no respect for the forests,

and silence the *adivasi* cultures that are built on this respect. But tribals themselves, caught in traps of poverty and powerlessness, can also lose respect for the forests and themselves clear and degrade their own resources.

The censorship of *adivasi* voices is subtle as well as deeply entrenched. There is no tradition of mutual dialogue: every tribe has its own language, with many strong dialects, completely distinct from India's numerous official languages. Apart from the few, and very junior, officials who come from a tribe, administrators virtually never speak one of these tribal languages.

Tribal languages are sophisticated, their speakers articulate. Expression is vivid, earthy, concrete, rich in metaphor and full of subtlety. Few outsiders ever hear or comprehend this discourse; even if they could understand the language, tribals themselves know all too well that most outsiders do not want to hear what an *adivasi* really thinks. Communication between *adivasi* and administrators, usually in the outsiders' language and with the help of interpreters, tends to follow a ritualised simplicity, such that outsiders speak of tribals as *sidha-sadha* 'straight and simple', and tribals, in turn, see outsiders as childlike in their superficiality. As a Durva saying puts it:'Outsider talk is baby talk.' Even without the problem of language, there is rarely the trust to speak openly to government officials. Again, as the Durva say:'The government has three qualities: to terrify, demand food and make the heart ache.'

In short, *adivasi* expect outsiders not to 'hear' them. When they speak to government officials, they often use the idiom of victims: 'We are poor', 'we have nothing' and so on, thus feeding the officials' stereotypes of tribals as destitute and without real cultures of their own whom they may have some obligation to help, but certainly no need to listen to. In the official mind, tribals are beyond the circle of relevant communication.

One hundred and fifty years ago, at the time of the first contacts between British officials or Hindu Rajas' representatives and tribal Elders, dealings were often full of elaborate respect. But, as the outsiders tightened their hold over *adivasi* and made use of an expanding police force, interaction became peremptory and exploitative. Bribe-extortion became commonplace and the trappings of the 'Saheb' role permeated dealings. Even in the early days, translators had the power to feed senior officials with the clichés they understood and expected. Rarely did anyone struggle with difficult and embarrassing 'other' ways of thinking.

With rare exceptions, and Madhu Ramnath is one of them, today's NGOs and anthropologists have done little to challenge the stereotypes and clichés of the past. While they do not view tribals as inherently inferior, many NGOs unwittingly act as a complex set of censors, or distorters, of a discriminatory discourse. As a medium for passing on a tribal view of life and an *adivasi* account of their own situation, the work of Indian anthropologists, in particular, is also of little use. ❏

Felix Padel *is an anthropologist whose work is centred on rural India. His most recent book is* The Sacrifice of Human Being *(1997, Oxford University Press)*

MADHU RAMNATH

Life and death in the forest

For 17 years, Madhu Ramnath has lived and worked as a botanist and anthropologist in Bastar, south-eastern Madhya Pradesh, the most remote and tribal area of central India. He speaks the Durva language: he has listened and learned from the people. The stories, poems and anecdotes that follow allow us, too, to listen to *adivasi* voices for the first time. They illustrate the state apathy that is common in the district and the level to which state-*adivasi* relations have sunk. They also show the resourcefulness of the *adivasi* in dealing with the unexpected – while the concept of a postmortem was a familiar one, suicide by hanging was new to the village

THE STORY OF NARSING MUTAK

The sun had not yet risen that winter morning when I heard the wail. Narsing Mutak's wife had come to the pond for water and saw her husband's body hanging from a branch of the large *kaldi* tree nearby. Her cry brought other people and I cut my walk short to join them. The *kotwal* and the other Elders arrived at the scene soon after and made the decision to report the matter at the police station an hour's walk away.

Nobody in the village went to work that day. We waited in our homes or near the *kaldi* tree. In the afternoon, a police superintendent accompanied by a constable arrived on a motorcycle to investigate. A *charpoy* (a low slung Indian-style bed), was brought out for the policemen and the men gathered on the sand some distance from the pond. The women and children watched from behind the fence of a nearby hut.

MADHU RAMNATH

Bhil dance at village feast, Gujarat – Credit: Ulli Steltzer

At the policeman's order N Mutak's wife and her two sons came forward and sat on the ground near the *charpoy*. The *kotwal* (headman), as wily as any *kotwal* in Bastar, hovered nearby. The inquiry began.

'So! You're the wife and you are the sons. Why did he go and hang himself?'

N Mutak's wife said she did not know. The sons said the same thing.

'A man does not go and hang himself for nothing. Give me a reason.'

'We don't know.'

'Motherfuckers! I want a reason.'

The corpse dangled from the tree behind us and every now and then, as relatives arrived from other villages, the wailing would gain new energy.

'Can't we say that he is truly a bad man who has not one woman to grieve him?'

The elder son replied that he hadn't a clue; that he had neither fought nor had an argument with his father.

'Look, you bastards, if I don't get a reason soon I'll take you to the *thana* (police station) and shove some bamboo up your arse. Then you'll talk.' Then he turned to the mourning relatives and shouted: 'Stop that noise!'

It went on in this fashion for sometime until the *kotwal*, quicker in these matters than the rest of us, whispered to us in Durwa. 'He needs something to put down in his *likha-padi*. Let's give him a reason.'

'Speak in Hindi, bastards!' The superintendent was instantly alert.

The sons of N Nutak began to speak about their father's limp that had kept him confined to the house for over a month. He had also had a painful elbow acquired during a fall; these injuries had caused him to use a stick to move about. Other people present began to contribute to the list of N Mutak's ailments, until it became obvious that the poor man was very sad and depressed. This satisfied the policemen who pulled out sheets of blank paper and a stamp pad, all prepared to get it over with. Five witnesses were called and their thumb impression taken on blank paper – the superintendent said he'd fill in their statements at the *thana* – and the atmosphere relaxed marginally.

'Let's take a look at the corpse.'

The men moved towards the tree. The policemen walked around searching for bloodstains, then measured the height from which the body was hanging, with the aid of a bamboo pole and a measuring tape.

'It's 10m 41cms,' the superintendent read out to the constable, who jotted it down.

'I think it's 10ft 4inches,' I put in gently.

'We will do it in Hindi, not *Angrezi* (English),' he said, and continued with his investigations. A little earlier, the superintendent had mentioned that the body would have to be taken to the dispensary, near the *thana*, for a postmortem. This was not suitable to the people as many relatives had already arrived for the funeral; moreover, they wanted the body to be buried in the village itself. After much haggling over the price, the policemen agreed that the doctor could be sent for and the medical inquiry could be performed in the village itself. Two boys were sent off to fetch the doctor.

Three men climbed up the tree to lower the body. It was placed on a mat and superficially examined when the doctor arrived on his scooter, accompanied by his assistant. The doctor rarely came to villages to visit sick people; he was known for his promptnesss in visiting the dead. The assistant immediately asked for a bottle of liquor which was brought to him. After gulping it down he hurried after the body which was being carried to the rocks in the northern part of the village.

The sun was low in the sky when the body was laid on a rock, with incense sticks planted in the ground around it. Most of the men were present but the women stayed back. The assistant, or *pot-padial* (stomach-ripper) as he is known in Durva, took up his rusty knife and a rock and set about his task. The doctor stood beside me and the policemen, and gave us a running commentary on the operation. The assistant slashed and ripped, shoving his hands in and out of the body, exposing different organs for the doctor's benefit. When the body was mutilated the doctor was satisfied that there had been no foul play.

'It's all right, you can break the skull now,' the doctor said.

The assistant took up the rock and smashed the skull. I asked whether that was necessary.

'In case of exhumation in the future,' I was informed. 'It is a sign that the PM has been done.'

The *pot-padial* then tied the body up with its insides still sticking out and announced that his job was over. A few relatives stepped in and covered the body with new cloth, a customary parting gift to the dead.

'Keep a few bits of new cloth for me,' the *pot-padial* called out, washing the blood off his hands. 'It's just a waste on the corpse.'

We tried to plead against it, me adding that I'd buy him much better cloth next day in the bazaar, but was ridiculed by the medical man. 'Don't be so soft! What's the use of all that cloth in the ground?'

The men and women could now proceed with the last rites. The policemen and the doctor walked away; the *kotwal* and a few of us were discussing the prices to be paid for their services. After some haggling the doctor agreed to Rs700, the assistant settled for Rs300 and the policemen wanted a large rooster and Rs80!

It was dark when the government finally left the village. We bathed and felt free to mourn the death of a lively man, who had amused us with his wit and song until the previous night.

DURVA SAYING

Aare undod bele nendiluk boja.
Wherever one sits, it's the earth that bears the burden.

BUTI'S REPLY, IN VERSE, TO MY QUESTION ABOUT WHAT SHE FELT ABOUT THE FOREST TODAY

What are they doing to the forest?
Clearing it, opening it
We have no more forest, no more woods to sit, to stand
My loved one, what can I say ...

Now, oh now
I don't find leaves, don't find firewood
From which forest shall we gather leaves
How shall we light the fire
Tell us, my loved one ...

This land is ours, this kingdom too
My younger brother. It's our forest, our woods
But the *sarkar* says it's theirs
But the land is ours, their kingdom too
It's we who give (the sacrifices), we who share it
But the *sarkar* claims it all, my loved one ...

Now, oh now
My younger brother
Outsiders come and say
Give us this and give us that
But we have nothing that we can give away (for free)
We want something in return

Now, oh now
My younger brother
They are *sarkari* people
When it comes to giving (the sacrifice) they say they are strangers
When it comes to sharing they say they are outsiders
But if we hadn't given, the strangers could not have eaten
If we had not shared, the outsiders could not have eaten
It's our land, it's our kingdom ...

They cheat the *adivasi*
And live
They live this way, they live that way
They cheat and they grab
They are strangers to our way ...

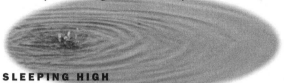

SLEEPING HIGH

It was a festival day in summer when most of the people in the village were imbibing *landa*, a fulfiling drink of fermented millet. Late in the morning, a group of us strolled over to the upper part of the village, for a change of taste and view. We made our way toward Lati's hut, hoping to get some toddy from his palm. A few weeks ago, Lati had slipped and fallen off another palm, twisting his hip. Since then it had been Hirma who tapped Lati's toddy for him.

We found Lati lying on a mat. He invited us into his fence and called out to his son to fetch some mats for us. After chatting a while, Lati sent his son to find Hirma; only the tapper knew the amount of toddy collected in the pot and if it had fermented enough.

The boy returned with the news that Hirma was not home: the tapper was somewhere in the village drinking *landa*! We said that we would drop in later and got up to leave, but Lati was keen for us to stay. He thought for a moment and spoke to his son. 'Climb up.'

Unga, Lati's son, was about 10 years old. Like all boys of his age he climbed palms, not to tap them but as a game, and took pride in it. On that particular day, he, too, had tasted *landa* from several pots, just like the rest of us.

We sat on the rocks under the palm, talking and watching Unga go up. Around his narrow waist he had secured the rope with which he would lower the gourd of toddy from the top. He reached the top and heaved himself up with the help of a frond, straddling it comfortably. He filled the gourd we sent him via the rope, then the gourd came down to us with the drink And then, still straddling the frond, the boy fell asleep.

Chatter beneath the tree stopped. As Lati watched from the mat, Mosu and Sombaru climbed up the tree. More rope was found and fashioned into an *utka*, a weave designed to bear heavy weights. Perched on adjacent fronds, Mosu and Sombaru gently fitted the *utka* around the sleeping boy. Then, after testing the knots, they lowered Unga carefully into the waiting hands below.

The boy was still asleep while we sat around him and quenched our thirst.

As far as the people could remember, this was the first time that someone had fallen asleep atop a palm tree. Yet, during the Unga incident, everyone near the palm could assess the urgency of the situation and responded instantly. No commands were issued. There was no sign of panic. Saving somebody's life is not so difficult, after all.

AN OFFICER COMES TO CALL

The afternoon sun was fierce and the village of Palob dozed. What little activity there was, was confined to the shade of large trees. The monotonous tuk-tuk-tuk call of the little coppersmith bird was broken by the distant hum of a vehicle. Before long, a red cloud in the distance was seen approaching the village. The jeep entered the village without pausing, making its way directly to my hut before coming to a halt.

People emerged from several huts and children peered from between the bamboo fences. A door opened and the senior officer (divisional forest officer), dressed like a Texan cowboy, scrambled out calling my name. Another door opened and the DFO's subordinates, a range officer and two forest guards in uniform, stepped out.

I invited them in, shooing the hen and her chickens away, and offered them mats to sit on. The senior man looked about him and entered hesitantly, seating himself awkwardly on the mat with his shoes on. The RO stood at the entrance, awaiting orders from his senior, while the two FGs ambled about my enclosed garden. The driver of the jeep remained in his seat.

'We have some to see what we can do for the people,' the senior man began. 'We want to take up some developmental works in the village.' Without really waiting for anyone's comments, he then proceeded to explain how he could improve agricultural conditions. Some money had

Bhilala family, Maharashtra – Credit: Ulli Steltzer

Simon Davies on

PRIVACY

Patricia Williams on

RACE

Gabriel Garcia Marquez on

JOURNALISM

Edward Lucie-Smith on

THE INTERNET

Ursula Owen on

HATE SPEECH

...all in INDEX

SUBSCRIBE & SAVE

UK and overseas

○ **Yes! I want to subscribe to *Index*.**

❏ 1 year (6 issues)   £39   Save 28%
❏ 2 years (12 issues)   £74   Save 31%
❏ 3 years (18 issues)   £102   **You save 37%**

Name _____

Address _____

_____ B9B4

£ _____ enclosed. ❏ Cheque (£)   ❏ Visa/MC   ❏ Am Ex   ❏ Bill me
(Outside of the UK, add £6 a year for foreign postage)

Card No. _____

Expiry   Signature

❏ I do not wish to receive mail from other companies.

INDEX   ✉ Freepost: INDEX, 33 Islington High Street, London N1 9BR
          ☎ (44) 171 278 2313   Fax: (44) 171 278 1878
          e tony@indexoncensorship.org

SUBSCRIBE & SAVE

North America

○ **Yes! I want to subscribe to *Index*.**

❏ 1 year (6 issues) $52   Save 21%
❏ 2 years (12 issues) $96   Save 27%
❏ 3 years (18 issues) $135   **You save 32%**

Name _____

Address _____

_____ B9B4

$ _____ enclosed. ❏ Cheque ($)   ❏ Visa/MC   ❏ Am Ex   ❏ Bill me

Card No. _____

Expiry   Signature

❏ I do not wish to receive mail from other companies.

INDEX   ✉ INDEX, 708 Third Avenue, 8th Floor, New York, NY 10017
          ☎ (44) 171 278 2313   Fax: (44) 171 278 1878
          e tony@indexoncensorship.org

Tribal fisherman, Narmada river, Madhya Pradesh – Credit: Ulli Stelzer

been assured to their department by the World Food Programme; a proposal had already been formulated and sent to the capital.

'Go get some people,' said the senior man to the RO.

'Go get some people,' said the RO to the FBs. The FBs wandered into the village.

In a short while, as the officer continued to explain his idea about 'progress and development' to me, the two FGs returned. With them came Birsu and Lambo, two Elders from the village, wondering what the whole thing was about. They had been lying in the shade and chatting. I welcomed them and offered them a mat.

'People's participation is very important,' said the officer to everyone in general. 'Yes sir,' agreed the RO. Birsu and Lambo sat to one side, continuing their chat in Durva, a language which none of the jeep people understood. And as the village people did not understand their peculiar mixture of English and Hindi, the officer mainly addressed the RO and myself.

'The most important thing is irrigation. We will build a dam and benefit everybody. Singh, find out where their stream is. Water is good for everybody, is it not?'

The last question was addressed to Birsu and Lambo. They looked about and guessed that they had to agree to something.

'Yes,' they said together, and continued their own conversation. They were making a joke about how sleepy they felt.

'Better variety of seeds for all the vegetables and crops,' droned on the official voice. 'And also saplings of fruit trees. At a later stage we will introduce wheat to the people.'

'Yes, sir.'

After this, the senior officer launched into his unique scheme of castrating all the bulls in Palob. A better breed of bulls will replace the present ones. Future cows in Palob will then yield litres and litres of milk.

At this point, old man Birsu dozed off and Lambo laughed and muttered, 'I'm going to fall asleep myself. What's he going on and on about?' I wanted to explain but did not know where to begin.

Then sounds of drunken talk, loud and punctuated with hiccups, approached us. It was Baya, my neighbour, who had been on a drinking spree all that week. He was speaking a mixture of Durva, Halbi and Hindi, and trying to get past the FGs blocking his path. Baya swore at them, suggesting incest; the children laughed and followed him towards my hut.

'What's all that noise?' The officer paused in his monologue.

Birsu awoke from his nap and rubbed his eyes.

'Just my neighbour dropping in,' I replied. 'Perhaps he wants a few words with you.'

'I think we have discussed everything quite well,' said the officer. He got to his feet hastily and banged his head against a low beam. 'The RO will look into the follow-up and keep me informed.'

'Yes, sir.'

They walked out and got into the jeep, each according to his designation. I received a brief farewell nod from the officer.

'Go.' This word was directed at the driver.

The vehicle came to life, reversed and bashed into my fence, then drove off. For a while we heard its hum, then all we could see was the red cloud receding.

We joined Baya for the rest of the afternoon.

THE WAY OF THE *PAIK*

Laikan's *kalthi* (threshing space) in the village of Palob, Bastar. Laikan, Ramdor and Ishwar are all between 35 and 40 years old.

Madhu: How do you feel when you see a *paik* (outsider, non-tribal)?

Laikan: I feel angry, I want to beat him up ...

M: Why?

L: Why?

Ramdor: We feed him and he ends up bossing us.

L: Whenever we meet one he addresses us as assholes ...

R: They shout, 'Motherfuckers! Is this your father's forest?' when they meet us in the forest.

Ishwar: They are so arrogant here, do they have so much forest where they come from?

M: No.

I: So they come to wherever there is a forest and claim it as theirs? They will finish this forest too ... How can these strangers come and say that this forest is theirs?

M: What should we do?

R: We need no forest guards here. Send them away.

L: We don't want *sarkari* (outsider) forest. Let the forest be ours alone. We can take care of thieves from other villages, we can tell them to create forests, and chase the *sarkar* away.

R: The *sarkar* can have its own forest in the city.

L: There used to be forest around the city in those days. We could find firewood to cook and spend the night there. But they have cleared everything now.

I: Our people looked after these forests for us, that's why we have them.

L: The forest is the only thing we need. Lots of forest and few people. Now it's the other way round, too many people.

M: What can we do to reduce the number of people? Kill some? (Pause and laughter)

L: Keeps happening ... but does not solve the problem. Look, the *sarkar* also tries to get us sterilised, so that we won't bear children, but people who have been sterilised still bear children, so many children that they make another village, and another ...

M: You mean sterilisation doesn't work?

L: It works for some, it has not worked for some...

I: Look at Baisaku, his wife still bears children.

M: Had he been for the operation?

R: He has: he has had three children after that.

I: And Warrak went from this part (of the village) ...

L: And Badhu from there ...

I: Badhu is going strong, he is a *mutak* (old man/Elder), still getting children.

L: It doesn't work for everyone.

I: Some of it manages to go across, all that love cannot disappear.

L: Where can all the love go? ❏

Madhu Ramnath has been associated with the people and forests of Bastar for 17 years. He is equally at home with Durwa knowledge and western science. He has never published or publicised his work. The conversations with the Durwa, as well as their songs and stories, were collected for this issue of Index

MARTHA DEMIENTIEFF

Ways of healing

A Yu'pik Elder from Alaska talks about her tribe's traditional medicine and respect for their fellow creatures

One time I had a dream. I was really wiped out, coming to the end of my schooling. I dreamed that I came to this campfire and a woman told me, 'Put that packsack down.' So I put it down. Then she said, 'Pick that thing up.' So I picked it up again and it was just light. When I woke up in the morning I felt really good. No more stress, no more pain, no more backache. I didn't know what to make of it so I went to her in a couple of days and told her: 'I dreamed about you.' She said: 'Don't tell no one.' I asked her why she helped me and she said that she didn't like to see young people suffer. So some would work on your dreams.

The healing really required some action on the part of the patient as well as the healer. Where I come from, a healer might tell me don't ever wear anything I have sewed. Don't eat these certain things, don't pick berries. If you did those things that they told you not to do, you would get sick again. There was one man whose back was so sore that he couldn't get up. He called several healers and they told him to use acupuncture. Not the kind of Asian acupuncture, but they used little blades. But he couldn't, because he was too scared. After, some other woman came over and she healed with touching and song. She massaged him and she sang her sacred songs. He got right up like there was nothing wrong with him. But she told him not to ever wear anything that she sewed. So he moved from there and got a job in another town. People from his hometown would come and when they came they would usually stay with him. One day, he said, his wife and one lady went downtown to visit. He was out on the sawhorse sharpening a saw. It was a nice spring day and he put on his visitor's slippers to go out and sharpen the saw. And he looked down the road and saw them coming and just fell right there. People had to carry him in, his back was so bad. They had him on the bed and were trying to help him. He looked at his feet and asked who made those slippers. It was the healer that made them! They took them off his feet and he was fine. So they had real restrictions. I don't know what the reason for that was. But he was in charge of his own wellbeing because if he didn't follow what she said he got sick again. Not everybody was like that. Each healer has their own gift and their own ways of healing.

This one woman who was healed was told never to pick berries again. This was a real burden on her life. We all had to pick berries for her because she was not allowed. I think this kind of restriction forces you to take part in your own healing ... In our language it's 'the thing that has two sides to it.' It's so good and yet it has a sinister side to it. ...

For every time that I have had a healing, I had to first ask for it then I had to do certain things, and I had to agree to that healing, and then during that healing I was not to be afraid. The way a healer from outside explained to me is, the creator doesn't want his grandchildren to be scared. If you're scared he won't go near you. So during the healing you have to try not to be afraid. So part of the healing is the healer uses lots of kind and comforting words. It's not a really scary thing like: 'Hold it! Breath!' It's all simple and soft. One time a healer said to me, 'What's the matter sister, did you fall asleep? Talk. Voice yourself.' I was having such deep feelings that I thought I was saying them but I was just sitting there with my mouth closed. He said: 'Sing! Do something, you fell asleep or what?' The humour in there too. It's not such a scary, serious thing ...

For me, in my life experience, the most healing experiences were, especially to calm and help with peace and harmony, a fire by the water. The mind opens up with that. Like this earth is going on as it should there is something eternal about fire and water, and the beauty of the earth. When I was in grief I couldn't understand how is it that the leaves turned green, how could the sun come up, how could the birds be singing? How come it's like nothing in this world is missing my husband. I was kind of mad at the way that the leaves turned green, the sun came up and the birds kept singing. But there was something reassuring about the permanence of it. When you sit by the fire and you hear the water, you know it's eternal. Things will be all right. For me it's like mother nature mothering you, reassuring you ...

A big brown animal that we're not supposed to say its name, kept bothering a family in Nulato. They couldn't scare it away, or chase it away, and they lived way at the edge of town. So, in order to protect his family a young man had to kill that thing. The law came and they took his guns, the animal, and had a trial and fined him, shamed him publicly. His mother started to cry, she said, 'Hah, a long time ago a young man who killed that big thing would be honoured by the whole community. It would be an honouring instead of a shaming.' Two different ways. That happens a lot. So I was trying to do that in the village, I would try to follow that. We also follow where we put the carcass. If it was a land animal, we have to put it away in a clean area of land. If was a water animal it has to go in the water with a prayer, 'More to come.' Asking that we will always receive this gift of fish or whatever. With the bigger, more important animals, you are not supposed to go back to that place where you placed them. Usually under a tree. You treat those places like a cemetery. They have to be respected. That is important to our well being. It frightens me to hear about people going to the Alaska Federation of Natives and there's a big debate about subsistence. Like it was an economic problem. In the old way the first thing we would do is examine our own spiritual condition. We should ask ourselves, am I talking about subsistence in a political way or am I actually living subsistence? Am I respecting that animal, being thankful, treating its bones the right way? It's no use to act like an expert and talk about subsistence in a political way. Once we separate the spirituality from our hunting and gathering practice we make it a political and economic issue. ❏

Martha Demientieff is a *Yu'pik Elder from Alaska*

MARTHA DEMIENTIEFF

Going away

In the spring, when the Yukon River is still frozen but thawing, the ice is dangerously thin. The young man, travelling by snowmobile to a down-river village to see his girl, breaks though the ice and is gone. The plan for a new family and a happy life are cut short and lost. The men search with sharp hooks to retrieve the body that must be put away the right way. The women pray and burn food at the grave site of the ancestors. The men succeed. The young man is found and the *potlach* is held, his song is made and he is buried with all the love and generosity that the village can provide, for there will not be another chance to give him anything again. When it is over the world should not be the same. How could it be for his mother Rose?

In summer, fishwheels are set in the swift Yukon River. A young man must check the salmon catch and bring it home for the women of the family to preserve for winter. The women are ready, knives sharp and fish-racks ready but he never returns. Maybe he broke down. Maybe he ran out of gas. The searchers return. His boat was found still tied to the fishwheel raft. He is gone. He must have slipped. The search begins again. The women pray. The prayers are answered. The hooks bring up the young man. The *potlach* is held, his song is made, the silence and finality of the burial is now. How can the world be the same again for his mother Mary?

In fall the migratory birds are leaving. For days we have seen and heard thousands of cranes, high overhead, going south. Mary looks up and angrily asks: 'Why they say that?'

The poem tells the rest.

Those cranes!
Why they say that.
They don't have to holler
When they're going away.
Why they say that?

Yea, my friend
Drink tea
You know they have to do that.
Our boys left
And said nothing.

But us we'll stay here.
After a while
We won't mind the cranes
When we pick berries
For our grandchildren.

Fall is lonesome
Right now nothing is good.
We have other kids.
Them too, they're sad.
Try to drink tea.

At least we got them back
From the water.
We said goodbye at *potlatch*.
Maybe crane too
Is crying for somebody. ❏

Martha Demientieff's 'Going away' *first appeared in* Descant *in 1993*

Tlingkit children, Alaska – Credit: Shorty Wilcox/Rex

TED CHAMBERLIN

A map of the world

From the silence of slavery came the voice of the Rasta

Repatriation. It's the watchword of our time. Ethnic cleansing, genocide, the terrors of civil war, the brutal conflicts between national sovereignty and racial or regional self-determination: these, we are told, are the special curse of our century.

But of the holocausts that haunt us – Jewish, aboriginal and African – it is the horror of African slavery that still seems the most difficult to bring to life in the imagination. Most of the the attempts to do so make it little more than what it always has been: a social and economic problem, a political embarrassment. None retain the sense of urgency that is felt by those who are still suffering.

Except Rastafari. Rastafarianism may be the only genuine myth to have emerged from settlement and slavery in the new world. It is a myth of origins and purposes, of beginnings and ends. It is a myth of dispossession and dislocation that draws on that other great account of racial and religious conflict, the Bible. It is where the sounds of the silence of slavery are given voice: in the music of reggae and rock–steady and its greatest singer, Bob Marley; and in the story told by his teacher, Ras Mortimo 'Kumi' Planno, greeting us in the name of the Imperial One, Emperor Haile Selassie I Conquering Lion of the Tribe of Judah, Jah Rastafari.

Rising above the violence of slavery, the treacheries of emancipation, and the recurrent antagonism towards Rastafarians, Brother Kumi celebrates the liberation of the spirit, the *bigging-up* of the self, that comes from breaking free (or 'braking free', as he says in one of the turns of language that characterise the 'dread talk' of Rasta) from not only the chains of slavery but also the compromises of Babylon.

'By the waters of Babylon we sat down and wept ... They that led us away captive required of us a song, and melody in our heaviness ... How shall we sing the Lord's song in a strange land?' asks the Biblical psalmist. We cannot, he implies ... and then, in a contradiction that goes to the heart of our finest imaginings of our most dreadful experiences, he goes on to sing that great song of sorrow and suffering. Out of Psalm 137 comes another, the anthem of Rastafari and the captivity of Africans in the Americas: 'By the Rivers of Babylon'. This is why there is the insistence on Repatriation in Brother Kumi's story of the Babylonian exile of his people. Rehabilitation means nothing more than better accommodation in Babylon.

Brother Kumi's voice is his own, and that of Jah speaking through him. But his imaginings call to mind those of another visionary, William Blake, whose prophetic writings still confuse and inspire, and of his contemporary Samuel Taylor Coleridge, arguing that the Bible contains 'a Science of Realities ... in which the Present involves the Future, and in the Finite the Infinite exists potentially'.

And where the Past is Present. This is where Brother Kumi's writing demands a radical imagining, the only kind that can resist the overwhelming pressure of reality. Babylon is not a metaphor for the world; the world is a metaphor for Babylon. Home is a metaphor for Africa. The earth is a metaphor for the Word. 'Peace and Love' is not a hope but a promise. Not a dream but a map. ❏

Ted Chamberlin is professor of comparative literature at the University of Toronto with a life long involvement in aboriginal issues. His latest book is Come back to me my language, Poetry and the West Indies

RAS MORTIMO 'KUMI' PLANNO

The earth most strangest man

Tell Out King Rasta Doctrines
Around the Whole World
Tell Out King Rasta Doctrines
Around the Whole World
Get your Bible and Read it
Read it With Understanding
Tell Out King Rasta Doctrines
Around the WHOLE WORLD
Zepheniah 3 Verse 9

Then Shall I Turn Unto they People
A Pure Language that They all may
Call upon THE NAME OF THE LORD
To Serve Him with One Consent.

Girmawi Kadamawi
Hyla Salase

Man's Immortality
Lives in His Progeny

Memories! They are like echoes, always come back. So, also with the Memories of Slavery ...

The Echoes of the Memories of Slavery resounded in the minds of the yet unborn of those who passes through the tribulation of Slavery. Truth can only be identified by Truth. So I approach the Haunting Memories of Slavery! I may caution here that I believe that Education should be a Right and not a privilege, yet I Education is limited as the Colonial System Represent. There is an old saying. 'They had to fool mi to Rule mi.' The British has completely fool our ancestors to Rule them. But we are made products of our own produce, by our acceptance of their Political System. Here is where I an trying to paint a picture that can be seen by even the Color Blind.

The British I an I Slavemaster write various conflicting Histories on African Slavery, lies, lies, lies, most of the Truth of African Slavery has been written in other foreign languages but not the British. I an I firmly know that Rulers were not made But were Born. In as, Men made Rulers days are numbered. But He who Born to Be Earth Rightful Ruler, will have to Rule or else the turn and overturn will never stop until whose Right He will get it. The British try to hide the identity of I an I by saying all the Slaves in Jamaica came from West Africa without Explaining the Market Sold East West and North and South African Slaves Sometime Asians and even Europeans. These confusing lies create an anxiety in I an I to learn more about Slavery and the British. I an I learn that King James vision of the Bible was given to I an I ancestors as valuable treasures of missionaries which was only a camouflage. The real purpose of the Bible was to christianize and civilize I an I ancestor. This system work for upward of 400 year's which seem to be I an I Sentence in this Pit of Hell. I an I ancestor worship with the Bible. I an I also worship from the Bible but do not worship the Bible. The Parson stand upon his pulpit and orate out lies like flies buzzing around the ears of his Congregation about a unknown God who have no meaning other than a Name until He is known. All these and many more will be surprising to the world to know How simple understanding can come to man. The faith of I an I is unbroken regardless of propaganda, So I an I will have to present and Represent I an I father Business, the Truth. The Bible was given finally, to our ancestors not before it was fully interpreted by Parson. But faith show I an I that words used can expound truth. WORD is Power and Power is God. The first Father in any Language I an I want to give to the world what is owed to them through the Mercy of I an I God. The Rastafarian all claim that they are Ethiopian one writer put it, and was so sure of his sentiment that they all want to go back to Ethiopia. By Ethiopia I an I mean one continent, by Ethiopia I an I mean the Country Ethiopia with its capital Addis Ababa. By Ethiopia I an I mean all for One, One for all operating in this manner there can be no failure. The only true interpretation for Africa for Africans. I an I being in captive Has to admit, to names of those who did pass through great tribulations: Such as Daniel, John, John the Baptist, Peter, Paul, David, Shadrack, Meshek and Abendego, Dreamer Interpreter and Dreadlock Rasta: All these names are Biblical, but there true identity has reproduces its manifestation. So I an I invite Human to a travel through Prophesies ...

I an I appear as the base things of the earth. I an I brethren live in rubbish dumps dunghills (Ghettoe's) cattle farming done by I an I was a creation to new generation. We move and had to move about So one would ask How I an I would manage not being steady. Hunting was a much appreciably sport for I an I, Hunting is the Second Nature of a Sheperd, I an I hunt for food as is always Man's demand the Hunt for food for the family. I an I has a household and a family, which stay Home and raise the family. I an I was created to proform this work for the kingdom Jesus Christ spoke of to come it sometime take I an I away from family life. So I an I live as Sojourners. I an I feel the spirit in I an I song.

> Leave our home and family
> to travel with the Lord of Love
> Leave our home and family
> to travel with the Lord of Love
> Travel, travel travel travel
> Travel with the Lord of Love.

The Loov of I an I the Loov of the Home, the Loov of the family the Loov of I an I cattle, all this Loov I an I sojourn with. I an I suffer for this Loov yet I an I suffage bring peace to many Nations Because I an I bloodshed to redeem many knowledge is power created and made yet knowledge cometh to those who seek after what History has written of Ethiopia is a stepping stone to the knowledge of the wealth of Ethiopia...

Man began to realise that Ethiopia is just not Ethiopia an undeveloped country but a special country which can be used as a pendulum to guide nations unto success ...

Words reach the throne Room that I an I were caught and captured and sold to foreigner's. The warning came that I an I should desist from going across the borders into another Territory for the pale face are making a good market in I an I as a product. I an I being warriors and statesman know that the duty of a sheperd is to defend. The king defence of his Empire remain inside the Empire. The time must come as it was in the beggining when the entire Continent come under the Kings of Kings and Lord of Lord's. His Imperial Majesty Haile Selassie I Emperor of Ethiopia The Resurrection of this disobedience was liken unto the warning unto the World Government Conscience in 1936.

> If you bow to force
> God and History will
> Record your Judgement.

These warning went unheeded, what happened? God and History Recorded the Judgement of Europe. I an I was not spared for such disobedience yet Rastafari send I an I down to Redeem Mankind by making I an I watchman upon the walls of Zion, I an I feel it in this Song:

> The Good Lord Send me from Zion
> The Good Lord Send me Down.

God revile himself unto Mankind yet Mankind Remove from his thought that God is Real. When the warning of God go unheeded then the visitation of his wrath kindled likened unto a fire ever burning. So also God send others to vilify and destroy the wicked who refused to obey. Slaves from Ethiopia always feel deep inside the Spirit of the African Movements and move to it in songs: as it is written in the Psalms of David To Every Song is a Sign and I an I always Sing the Songs of the Signs of the Time:

> Run away Run away Run away
> Haile Salassie I call you
> Bright angels are waiting
> Bright angels are waiting
> To carry the tiding Home
> Blackman.

Nothing more true than the Spirit of the Rastafarians Movement to move away from Jamaica or any other land to Ethiopia for I an I sing:

> Ethiopia is a better land
> Ethiopia is a better land

> Ethiopia is a better land
> Oh yes Rastafari oh Yes

I an I know that the light shine and the slave master was able to see it. I an I came down in San Salvador the Bottom-less pit. But I an I God who I an I serve swore unto I an I with a oath promising I an I to come down to visit I an I in the pit of Hell. All this took time to manifest but it was written That the isles must wait upon His law. I an I waited and He came to the Isles and I an I was satisfied while pale face were vilified other I an I cannot describe, Saw H.I.M and say Truth. Seen?

THE BIBLE INTERPRETED BY I AN I

I an I am aware of the many doctrinal denomination. All have a bible system. God become meaningful to some while others, began doubting the ideas of God and his Power's. King James of England 1066 Translate the Bible in English Considering that World Power was given unto England by the consent of Europe. yet Britain Intelligence fail in many perspective. I an I know that the Problem to know the living God came in the Misinterpretation of Scriptures which is written yet now learned ...

Students and learned intellectuals who are ognastics have and produce many arguments in support of there disbelief in the theory of God and the Authority of the Bible. I an I get a solace from the words of the Bible: for words in any Language is what count. The most important thing about I an I is the way I an I interpret the Bible as Rastafarians...

Those in the churches preaches that God is the word. I an I accept. In the churches I an I learn that God have many names which he is so called. Yet I an I was only allow to use the name that satisfy the church, yet still there is a doctrine of the church which said my name shall be terrible and dreadful amongst them I an I chant this chant in this time to fulfill this line:

> A new name you got
> And it terrible amongst them
> The heathen no like you name
> A new Name you got
> And it dreadful amongst them
> The heathen no like your Name.

Such name I an I say Shout it out if you are not a heathen:
RASTAFARI: RAS-Fa-Ta-Ri
Girmawi Kadamawi Hyla Silase.

THE NOW-RASTAFARIAN

The name is attach to Brethren of the movement according to certain sentiment. The name Ras-Fa-Tar-i is the proper pronunciation which is an Amharic word, meaning Head-Creator, Ras (Head) Fa Tari (Creator) His Imperial Majesty – Being Born in wedlock, His family name Makkonen. He became Ras which is an Ethiopian title of the military a head, Synonomous to a General in the British Army, Ta-Fari was given as a Blessing. Haile Selassie I is an enbeded name written upon His tigh on his vesture. When H.I.M. time of Birth it was like a blessing for the coming of H.I.M. broke the Dry Season which the rain brought with it the message of a Son who is Born and was given as a child, and his name shall be Called Blessed, The Mighty God, The Everlasting Father, The Prince of Peace, and in his Reign there shall be no end and in his Reign all the Govt's shall be upon his shoulder. What more evidence one want to see all African in particular and the world in general Govts is on the shoulder of His Imperial Majesty the Prince of Peace. His Reign shall have no end is likened unto the Two system of Ethiopia in as much. Axsum was and is The Ancient Kingdom of Ethiopia which saw the Histories of the various Kings of the Kingdom. Menelek prophesied that in Finifini the New Flower. This New Capital shall be Establish, Addis Ababa the Beginning of Prophesis which establish a new name in it self. Menelek II being the last Emperor of Axsum. Haile Sellassie I Became the first Emperor of the New City Capital Addis Ababa. This New Name of the city and its Emperor charm many when such Name has been Glorified. Jealously spring fort when the Name of Ras Ta Fari has been mention...

Many things have been said of the Rastafarian Movements ... I an I wanted to know more about Marcus Garvey Since he had advocated Repatriation back to Africa. I had to satify Self of How this could ever be done. I realizes that all can be achieve by the determination of a people to cite Law's that were made especially for them I started thinking upon certain lines. How one can be born in Jamaica and claim to be an African and need Repatriation to Africa. This Question as puzzling as it may Sound the answer was very easy: *Slave's were taken away from Africa Some forceably while other were bought and Sold.* To accept that I an I the product of Slavery gave I an I The Right to Speak as an African ... The Strangeness of the Rastafarian Manerism Can be Sum up into three words 'They are Africans'...

'BRING MY SONS from a far and my Daughters from the ends of the Earth. Even everyone that is called by my Name' called by which Name? which Name I an I are called? 'Rastafari' I an I are those people. I an I need no force of Arms to simple say give up. I an I remove from one stage to the other in philosophies and doctrines. The African people abroad had answered the clarion Call of the Earth Most Strangest Man. The Rebel Christian. The Schools The Churches The Univercities all Govt institutions of teaching and Learning are called upon to study these factors of Realities. I an I do not prepare to approach it less Simple than chose between Right and Wrong when find out. This Right and Wrong Knowledge causes Mans understanding to unite when face with the Realities of Peace and War. Man have to War within and without himself to approve and disapprove of the Conditions that create such situation that lead to these problems of Misunderstanding. I an I is not going to the Promise land that did not coincide with the text. 'In my fathers House there is Many Mansions' If it were not so I would have told you.' To See Through the glass at the realities of I an I through Law will enable all people to come forth Representing truth. Then only then there will be peace.

All the brethren want to be repatriated to ETHIOPIA. There is no agreement, however, on what should happen in the meantime. The majority recognise that they have to live, and would welcome efforts to provide employment, housing, water and other amenities. There is, however, a very vocal minority which regards any effort to help Ras Tafari brethren in these ways as a plot to keep them in Jamaica. They profess themselves to be violently opposed to any measures which might have the effect of rehabilitation ...

Colonialism is only Another name for Slavery and if our Leaders fail from Seeing how close they are taking us back to this Slavery it would be time to Start think in a different perspective. It take a lot of Sacrifices to overcome the obsticles which is set before the entire African People. Let us all Commit ourselves of learning from the Pass, what I an I have done why we are to be brought into Slavery and when the time Come for us to be free we notice another type of Slavery ...

How I an I view the entire issue of Repatriation Cannot easily balance with a peace and Loov-Doctrine only. The Time has Come when I an I have to challenge Mankind with the Power of God ...

I an I know that now is the time when Strange things have to happen, that can not easily comprehended by lay people. But the Principalities of the world are in turmoils to seek the hidden wisdom of the Earth Most Strangest Man. The Rastaman. A seed which serves the Generation and began to serve the yet unborn of our Race of People. The heteragenuisy of the Rastafarian Movement can some what be attached to the independent opinion of the individual which is a freedom of ones opinion without interference. One's mind function upon the type of mediation one illculcate under certain environment. Peace and Love is a virtue not inseperable virtues, but a virtue which embraces conditions. Peace is a condition, which is applicable, and most needed in the world. ❏

Ras Mortimo 'Kumi' Planno *is a Rastafarian Elder living in Jamaica.* The Earth Most Strangest Man *is a short excerpt from an unpublished book-length manuscript of the same name written in the 1980s and later transcribed by Lambros Comitas, director of the Research Institute for the Study of Man, New York*

GESSO

The way I understand it

'I have had a dream,' says Gesso. 'A dream, not a vision that would have come with its own authority to tell me my destiny.' Then his words emerged like a landscape from the fog and fell into the shape of a poem ...

It's a dream I have had
A dream with neither head nor tail
whose meaning escapes me a little.

Perhaps it shows without saying
that I am meeting you and telling you
before finding its place
in the meaning of its own story?

An old medicine-man was standing there.
But where had I already met him?
I could not see clearly.

Then I opened my eyes with determination
A large truck was approaching along the road,
there were three people on board
who were speaking in a strange language.

But it was me who was there in their midst.
How could I understand these languages?

I then climbed down into the inside of myself
entering quietly through my eyes
and entering this new country.

The truck was heading south,
south-west in fact, to the desert;
some mountains, far off,
already were profiled on the horizon.

I looked around myself
moving along in the truck.
The medicinal plants that
I was in the middle of eating,
I had already swallowed some,
I was absolutely sure of it.

You were about fourteen years old
my dream told me, explaining
that you had gone into the desert
for the first time.

I had so wanted to go into the desert
since my earliest childhood
believing that I was going to walk
for the first time in my life.

And there my dream revealed to me
that I had already been in a life
that came and went as it pleased.

A life that flew like a bird
on each side of me, like that,
overtaking me or letting itself be overtaken.

Perhaps that's why
my dream woke itself up
right in the middle of unfolding.

This dream that I tell you
was its one aim
to put me face to face
with the sense of having already seen
that which I looked for without knowing it?

This sense of *déjà-vécu* (a former life)
which we fall into sometimes
with such intensity along a dream
and which never gets explained!

Why does one know already
that which one sometimes discovers
and without being able to explain it?

Why does one often forget
but not always these places
already travelled in another life?

And where is the source of my obsession
with motorbikes,
me an Iroquois from the forest?

★★★

I have all sorts of bars within me.
In 1990, I had a severe motorbike accident
but I didn't pass away for some reason.

Maybe you don't consider death is a limit
But had I not been a biker or a Native American
I would have had a better job for sure
but might have entirely missed out my art
You're not limited to one dice after all
and everyone is endowed with the power
of coming back, to be born again.

It's when you travel across North America that the spirit of your ancestors begins more and more to make you aware and to talk to you. But the curtains of noise and pollution that cripple all communication must be lifted. Because, sooner or later, men will have to decide if they want to perish or survive and therefore try to rediscover the old and antecedent language that, one day, can allow the ancestors freely to take care of the land and the earth. Song-language that has hidden itself somewhere in the secret place that they have called 'the red man'. ❏

Gesso, *also known by his Iroquois name* **KaroniaKeson** *and his Canadian alias* **Harold Thomas**, *was a painter and motorcyclist who died in 1998. The above excerpt is from an interview with Jean Morisette under the title* 'The way I understand it or Trying to find a place to pray in peace'

TRIBAL LIFE: STATISTICS

European colonialism has caused the deaths of at least 50 million tribal people. The displacement of tribal peoples by modern farmers and 'developers' has contributed to the loss of 2,000 languages.

> *'Such as have been taken young and well treated, have turned out most excellent servants...'* J. Barrow, traveller and writer, speaking of the Hottentot of the Cape, 1801.

▌ 6,000 languages are spoken today. 3,000 of these are endangered. Eighty per cent of endangered languages are spoken by indigenous peoples . Linguists predict the loss of these within the next generation.

▌ The Australian Aborigine population was about one million when Europeans arrived; in 1930, it was 30,000.

▌ In 1600 Bushmen occupied all but the coastal strip of what is now South Africa. By 1990 the last Bushman community lived as squatters at the edge of the Kalahari.

> *'The wave of European colonisation was not to be stayed from rolling on by a few savages who stood in its course.'* G.M. Theal, historian of Africa, 1919.

▌ In 1974 the last Bushman language of South Africa was declared extinct.

> *'A boor from Graaf Reynet being asked ... if the savages were numerous or troublesome on the road, replied, he had only shot four.'* J. Barrow, speaking of the Bushman, 1801.

▌ Between 1904-1907, colonial aggression in Namibia and Tanzania killed approx. 350,000 members of tribal communities.

▌ Africa contains 10 per cent of the world's population but one third of its languages. All the hunter-gatherer languages of Africa are at risk.

▌ Between 1950-1991, experts estimate that 8,500,000 tribal people in India have been displaced by developement.

*T*he *heart that beats within a Kond is dark and ignorant, a very wildness, like the trackless waste in which he hunts his game ... This moral jungle must be levelled, the soil prepared to receive the seed, and the early and latter rains must fall thereon.'*
Goverment Report, India, 1863

■ Sri Lanka was once the land of the Vannialla-Atto hunters and gatherers. Only 2,000 remain. Until 1988, Sri Lankan governments excluded even these survivors from their lands.

> *'Of anything they have, if they are asked for it, they never say no, on the contrary they invite the person to share it and display as much love as if they would give their hearts.'* Christopher Columbus in his first report to Ferdinand and Isabella of Spain, 12 October, 1492.

■ In what became the United States indigenous population fell from 8 million in 1490 to 800,000 in 1890. 11 million native Americans died in the first 80 years following the Spanish invasion of Mexico. Within a century of European arrival, tribal population in Brazil fell from 2,500,000 to 225,000.

■ In Canada, 90 per cent of the Haida Nation died in 19th-century smallpox epidemics. In 1995, the Haida people won a claim to part of their traditional lands.

■ 25% of Canadian-Indian children going to residential school in the 1900s died at the school or shortly after returning home. In the 1990s charges were brought against teachers at residential schools. Several have been found guilty of abuse.

■ 75 per cent of land in British Colombia is claimed by First Nations as theirs.

■ In April 1999, the Inuit of Canada secured Nunavut, the first modern indigenous administration.❑

Benefit of silence

The woman explained the tragedy that had befallen two families from the Decani region of Kosovo. It was her job to lead her family's half of the negotiations that traditionally precede the marriage of a Kosovo Albanian couple.

But in January the engagement was broken off. A messenger brought news that the bride-to-be had been snatched a week earlier by three policemen. One had raped her. 'We are an honourable family,' the messenger said, 'and do not wish to cheat you.'

'She will never again see the light of day,' the woman said, 'and will die an old woman in her parental house.'

Rape victims in Kosovo are victims twice over, because of the Code of Leke Dukajini, a body of fifteenth century customary law that still holds sway in Albania and Kosovo. The code covers all social activity, from the role of the church and care of livestock through to marriage and, that most male of matters, 'honour'. A man who fails to exact blood revenge for the dishonour of his womenfolk brings shame on the entire family.

Serb paramilitaries used rape to target families of supporters of the Kosovo Liberation Army (KLA), fully aware of the devastating effect the rapes would have on the fighters and their communities. First reports of the strategy emerged from Likosani and Cirez in the district of Drenica where women were detained on 27 February and held for 48 hours. A week later, some 200 people were held in an arms factory in Srbica. There, according to one witness, young women were separated from the group and assaulted.

The reports continued for months. In October masked paramilitaries surrounded a group of young people from Ljebusa as they picked chestnuts near Decani monastery. They beat up the boys and took away a 15-year-old girl. Released an hour later, there was no hiding her ordeal. She was scratched and weeping and her hair had been slashed off with a knife. Her entire family packed up and left for Montenegro the following day.

According to the Code of Leke, a woman raped in front of her own family is expected to commit suicide. If not, the shame ripples outwards. The victim becomes a prisoner in her own home and even her sisters may end up spinsters because of the humiliation. Married victims can be forced out of the home, even if they have children.

In the face of this harshness, Kosovar women fight to keep their ordeals secret. A woman who helped a neighbour whose two daughters-in-law were raped near Pec last November vowed to keep the attack secret. 'I didn't tell anyone and neither did the mother-in-law. Their husbands do not know about the rape. If they did, they would have forced them out of the home immediately.'

Journalists and human rights activists only lately came to understand the scale of the atrocity. Few realised that the systematic use of rape – as practised during the Bosnian war – was repeated in Kosovo. Investigators tended to draw a blank. The women detained in Jabukovo Polje in Drenica last September say only that they were 'threatened' and questioned – nothing more.

Even in Vranic, where a group of women was raped last September, the victims strenuously deny the attack. Only one elderly woman would speak. 'I saw a lorry-load of raped women taken to the station in Suva Reka. One of the women whom I knew said only: "It would have been better if I had been killed".'

Finally, what of the perpetrators? Hopes that they may one day be brought to justice are slim. Thousands of Muslim women were held in the 'rape camp' in the Bosnian town of Foca. The International Criminal Tribunal in The Hague indicted nine of their attackers. One went voluntarily to face trial in The Hague and another was shot dead during an attempt by western SFOR troops to arrest him.

The others are still at large, freely walking the streets of Foca. ❑

Gordana Igric is a senior editor with the Institute of War and Peace Reporting who has investigated rape as a war crime in Bosnia and Kosovo.

A censorship chronicle incorporating information from the American Association for the Advancement of Science Human Rights Action Network (AAASHRAN), Amnesty International (AI), Article 19 (A19), the BBC Monitoring Service Summary of World Broadcasts (SWB), the Committee to Protect Journalists (CPJ), Canadian Journalists for Free Expression (CJFE), Glasnost Defence Foundation (GDF), The UN's Integrated Regional Information Network (IRIN), the Inter-American Press Association (IAPA), the International Federation of Journalists (IFJ/FIP), the International Federation of Newspaper Publishers (FIEJ), Human Rights Watch (HRW), the Media Institute of Southern Africa (MISA), International PEN (PEN), Radio Free Europe/Radio Liberty (RFE/RL), Reporters Sans Frontières (RSF), the World Association of Community Broadcasters (AMARC), World Association of Newspapers (WAN), the World Organisation Against Torture (OMCT) and other sources

ALGERIA

The independent daily *Demain L'Algérie* was prevented from printing its 16 May edition, allegedly for 'non-payment of debts'. Most Algerian printing houses are owned by the state which often uses non-payment of debts as a pretext for stifling criticism. The same argument was cited for the closure of *La Nation* in December 1996. (*Index* 1/1996, 3/1996, 6/1998). (RSF)

ANGOLA

William Tonet, director of the weekly newspaper *Folha 8*, was interrogated by the Criminal Investigation Department for several hours on 6 April about his informants within the army following a legal proceeding brought against him by the military high command. Tonet was accused of inciting young men against enlisting, incitement to desert and slander against the army. (Media Institute of Southern Africa)

On 10 April a complaint was lodged against **Gustavo Costa**, correspondent for Portugal's *Expresso* magazine, following publication of his article alleging billing fraud by those close to President Dos Santos, including his daughter. The complaint against Costa, an Angolan citizen, could have implications for the twice-weekly *Agora* newspaper which, in its 10 April edition, reported the same story in an article entitled 'Corruption is creating victims'. (RSF)

On 28 April **Josefa Lamberga**, of the Luanda bureau of the Voice of America, was hit twice in the face by a soldier while attempting to report on draft evasion at a military recruiting centre in the city. Lamberga claims the attack was in revenge for a report of hers that claimed that 'mulattos' were escaping the draft at the expense of blacks. (CPJ)

ARGENTINA

On 31 March the Inter American Commission on Human Rights decided to examine accusations related to three judgments of the Supreme Court affecting freedom of expression: the sentence against actress **Gabriela Acher** and television station Channel 13 (*Index* 1/1999); one against **Tomas Sanz**, editor of *Humor* magazine (*Index* 2/9999, 3/1999); and the indefinite extension of the suit of Minister of Interior Carlos Corach against Verbitsky. (Periodistas, RSF)

On 8 April journalist **Eduardo Kimel** was sentenced to a one-year prison term and a US$20,000 fine for defaming judge Guillermo Rivarola in his book *La Masacre de San Patricio* (The San Patricio Massacre). The book criticised the judge for not having sufficiently investigated the 4 July 1976 assassination of five persons by death squads, a crime that remains unpunished. In November 1996 the Court of Appeals overturned a verdict one year earlier which ruled that the incriminatory passages were not defamatory. Judge Rivarola appealed the decision and asked for the case to go for retrial. (Periodistas, RSF) **Check back issues**

Ricardo Gangeme, editor of the weekly magazine *El Informador Chubutense*, was shot dead on 13 May while parking his car in front of his apartment. The perpetrator escaped on foot in spite of the rapid arrival of the police. *El Informador Chubutense* was well known for reporting on local corruption. (Periodistas, Freedom Forum)

ARMENIA

The independent newspaper *Oragir* is refusing to pay US$25,000 in compensatory damages to the Mika Armenia trade company, the paper's editor-in-chief, **Nikol Pashinian**, announced on 16 April. A Yerevan court levied the damages a day earlier for 'tarnishing the reputation' of the company, which is linked to Interior Minister Serzh Sarkisian. In March, *Oragir's* lawyers failed to persuade a court that it had been libelled by Sarkisian. (*Index* 2/1999). (RFE/RL)

The Central Election Commission (CEC) decided in mid-April to allow each of the 21 parties registered for the 30 May elections to air 60 minutes of political messages free on state television, and a further two hours at a cost of only US$5 per hour. The CEC mandated that an on-screen counter should show each party's cumulative time on air. By 5 May, state TV had conceded that it lacked the technical means to present a cumulative counter and would have to keep a paper tally instead. (RFE/RL, Noyan Tapan)

AZERBAIJAN

Qanun magazine journalist **Rovshen Ismayilov** was arrested while trying to buy bread at his local market on 13 April. He was taken to Nizami District police station, where he was beaten and held in the cells for two days. He was charged with resisting arrest and then released. (Azerbaijan Trade Union of Journalists)

On 21 April the justice ministry rejected the Trade Union of Journalists' (TUJo) November registration request on the grounds that it is a 'political organisation'. The ministry asserted that the TUJo is dominated by opposition newspapers although, in fact, pro-government media workers are also members. The rejection follows the ministry's refusal last August to recognise TUJo's precursor, the Labour Union of Azerbaijani Journalists, on the grounds that its name and charter were not 'written in Azeri language', apparently code for the use of Turkish words rather than Arabic or Persian ones. (Azerbaijan Trade Union of Journalists)

On 30 April reporters **Vefa Allahverdiyeva** of *Sharq* and **Azer Sariyev** of *Express* were harassed by parliamentary deputy Ahad Abiyev and his bodyguards. Abiyev, who was angry at what Allahverdiyeva had written about him, accosted her following a session of the Milli Mejlis (Parliament). When Sariyev tried to intervene, the deputy attempted to hit Sariyev and then ordered his bodyguards to throw both journalists out of the building. In the event a bystander persuaded the bodyguards to relent. (Azerbaijan Trade Union of Journalists)

An international campaign to release **Fuad Gahramanly**, the country's only imprisoned journalist, was launched on 5 May by the International Press Institute and other organisations. Gahramanly is serving an 18-month prison sentence for an alleged 'call to social disorder' contained in an unpublished article seized during a 16 June 1998 Interior Ministry raid on the offices of the independent newspaper *Chag*. After the paper's editor and deputy editor were detained by police seeking the article's author, Gahramanly turned himself in on 18 June and was sentenced on 27 November (*Index* 1/1999). While in prison, Gahramanly contracted hepatitis. On 27 May some 50 people picketed the Supreme Court building in Baku to demand Gahramanly's release. (Azerbaijan Trade Union of Journalists, International Press Institute , CPJ, RFE/RL)

The press came under attack twice on 24 May, both times while police were ostensibly dispersing political rallies. *Uc Nogte* reporter **Mahir Resuloglu**, covering a Musavat Party youth rally outside the Milli Mejlis, was beaten by police and had his press card confiscated. Later in the day, police attempting to disperse a march by the Popular Front Party ended up attacking a building that houses the *Azadliq* and *Chag* independent newspapers and Turan news agency. *Azadliq* deputy editor **Rovshen Hajiyev** and *Tezadlar* correspondent **Allahverdi Donmez** were beaten by police. (Azerbaijan Trade Union of Journalists)

Recent publication: *Mass Media in Azerbaijan* (Yeni Nasil

Journalists' Association, May 1999)

BAHRAIN

The trial of the writer and scholar **Sheikh al-Jamri** (*Index* 3/1995, 4/1995, 6/1995, 2/1996, 3/1999) has not resumed since the death of erstwhile ruler Sheikh Issa on 6 March. Al-Jamri, 62, was arrested on 20 January 1996, in connection with a petition he circulated calling for a return to constitutional government, and held for three years without charge until his trial began on 25 February. (WiPC, PEN, Bahrain Human Rights Organisation)

BANGLADESH

During a national strike on 11 May baton-wielding policemen attacked photo-journalists **Borhanuddin** of *Manobjamin*, **Habib** of *Ajker Kagoj*, **Emran** of the *Daily Star*, **Abutaher Khokan** of the *Financial Express*, **Joy** and **Farid** of *Janakantha*, **Sanaul Haq** of the *Independent* and **Khaled Haider** of *Dinkal* after they tried to photograph police assaulting a woman opposition activist. Later that day, photographers **Tapan Dev** of *Khabar*, **Gulam Mustapha** of *Sangram* and reporters **Azmal Haq Helal** of *Matribuni* and **Ziaur Rahman Madhu** of *Banglar Bani* were hit by rubber bullets. (Media Watch)

BELARUS

On 14 April **Syarhey Antonchyk**, an independent trade unionist and head of the Strike Committe, was fined 10 million Belarusian roubles (US$41.50) for 'organising and holding an unsanctioned rally' at a plant in Orsha in early March. Antonchyk claimed he only conversed with workers, a position confirmed in statements from plant staff and two policemen. (RFE/RL)

On 17 April police arrested **Tadeusz Gawin**, chairman of the Union of Poles, for organising an unsanctioned picket in Hrodna. Protestors brandished posters blaming central and local authorities for 'suppressing the Polish educational system'. (RFE/RL)

BOSNIA-HERZEGOVINA

The Independent Media Commission (IMC), composed of local and western 'media experts' and set up to vet news standards in the divided republic, ordered Kanal S to stop broadcasting on 15 April. The IMC deemed that the Pale-based station – sometimes referred to as 'Karadzic TV' – had covered the Kosovo conflict in an 'inflammatory and systematically inaccurate' manner. (CPJ)

BURKINA FASO

The Independent Commission of Inquiry investigating the death of journalist **Norbert Zongo** on 13 December 1998 (*Index* 1/1999) concluded on 7 May that Zongo was 'assassinated for purely political motives because he practised investigative journalism.' The Commission's 35-page report failed to find sufficient evidence to identify the guilty parties, although a list of 'likely culprits', including six soldiers from the presidential security regiment, was put forward. (RSF, PanAfrican News Agency)

Halidou Ouédraogo, president of the human rights organisation Mouvement Burkinabé des Droits de l'Homme et des Peuples, was arrested and detained for two hours on 17 May. On 10 May his home had been surrounded by a group of over 100 people who threatened and insulted him. Opposition leader **Hermann Yaméougo**, also arrested on 17 May, remains in custody. (AI)

CAMEROON

There are fears for the safety of **Amié Mathurin Moussy**, editor-in-chief of the newspaper *La Plume du Jour*, which has been suspended since September 1997. After an interview with the French radio station Fréquence Paris Plurielle on 23 May, police officers visited his house in Douala. The men asked to see the journalist and left after having interrogated several family members. Moussy was due to return to Cameroon on 27 May. (RSF)

CHILE

All 1,200 copies of the *Black Book of Chilean Justice*, written by investigative journalist **Alejandra Matus Acuna**, were confiscated by police the day after its launch on 13 April. The Court of Appeals considers the book insulting to the authorities and, therefore, a 'crime against public order'. The journalist immediately flew to Buenos Aires to avoid arrest. Matus is the fourth author since 1993 to fall foul of the State Security Law which empowers judges to ban texts if they are suspected of offending public officials. (IFJ, CPJ, HRW, Freedom Forum)

CHINA

The China News Publishing Agency banned further sales of a biography of Fidel Castro by a historian at the Chinese Academy of Social Sciences on 26 March. All 8,000 copies of *The Last Revolutionary of the Twentieth Century* were recalled in response to a complaint from the Cuban embassy that the book 'hurt [Cuba's] image'. (Associated Press)

On 30 March the authorities announced new restrictions on foreign tourists travelling to Tibet. Tourists in Lhasa must now be 'escorted' at all times by an officially approved guide, regardless of whether they are part of an organised tour. The Lhasa Tourism Bureau attributes the changes to 'traffic problems'. (Agence France Presse)

On 9 April police warned reformist political thinker **Bao Tong** (*Index* 6/1990, 8/1990, 4/1992, 2/1995, 4/1996, 4/1997) that his letter to the leadership, calling for a reversal of the official verdict on the Tiananmen Square massacre, 'endangered state security'. The government maintains that the army intervention was an 'appropriate response' to 'a counter-revolutionary rebellion'. (HRW)

Ma Xiaoming, a journalist for a local television network in Shaanxi Province, was detained on 15 April while covering a farmers' protest over tax in the Zhizou area. Ma renounced his Communist Party membership following his arrest in 1998 for giving an interview to the Voice of America during US President Bill Clinton's visit to China. (RSF)

On 11 May four dissidents were arrested at the anti-NATO demonstrations in Beijing for attempting to distribute leaflets calling on the government to pay reparations to the families of the victims of the bombing of the Chinese Embassy in Belgrade. **Cao Jiahe**, editor of newspaper *Dong Fang*, was released on 14 May after four days in prison during which he was beaten and deprived of sleep. It was reported that **Gao Wei** and **Yu Zhembin** have been released but there is no news on the whereabouts of the fourth dissident **Lu Guangwen**. On 26 May **Wang Wenjiang** and **Wang Zechen**, two dissidents who planned to petition the government to change its stance on the Tiananmen Square protests of 1989, were detained by police in the province of Liaoning. Police reportedly detained over 50 activists in the run-up to the anniversary, among them: **Jiang Qisheng** from Beijing, a student leader of the 1989 demonstrations, on 12 May; **Li Bagen** from Hangzhou city, member of an outlawed democratic opposition party, on 17 May; **Zhang Paoqin** of Fujian province on 26 May; and

Kong Youping of Anshan province on 27 May. (Agence France Presse, Associated Press, HRW, Reuters)

Around 500 Christians in Xian, central China, clashed with police on 23 May over the demolition of the city's oldest church. The Patriotic Protestant Associaton sold the church to a property developer after increasingly large congregations, occasionally numbering 2,000 to 3,000 worshippers, began attending. The proceeds have been spent on a new church but its location in a distant suburb has caused 'great dissatisfaction' among the city's Christians. (Agence France Presse, Fides, Reuters)

On 24 May the *Press Digest* reported that authorities had detained 71 members of the Mentu Hui religious sect in Chongqing in southwest China in April. The sect was declared an illegal organisation in the wake of President Jiang Zemin's declaration of a war on cults in January. (Reuters)

Three labour activists from a transportation company in Tianshui city, Gansu province, were charged with subversion on 27 May for organising a workers' rights group and accepting funds from an unspecified US-based organisation. **Yue Tianxiang, Guo Xinmin** and **Wang Fengsheng**, who had demanded that workers be paid salaries up to three years in arrears, were arrested on 11 January following the formation of a union group. (Agence France Presse, Reuters)

The tenth anniversary of the Tiananmen Square massacre on 4 June was marked by a few isolated gestures in Beijing which were quickly suppressed. 'Resurfacing work' conveniently blocked off the main area of the square, but a young man made a brief dash across the margins scattering leaflets which urged people to 'rise up and ... build a just new China' – before he was arrested. A middle-aged man was detained for raising an umbrella bearing slogans commemorating the pro-democracy demonstrations. In the run-up to 4 June, the government suspended the issuance of permits under the National Demonstration Law, introduced after the 1989 crackdown. On 28 May 50 dissidents, led by **Wang Rongqing** of the banned Democratic Party, had their application for a permit rejected by city authorities in Hangzhou. On 1 June the Public State Bureau cut access to CNN and other international channels until 8 June, ordering hotels and apartment blocks to stop satellite broadcasts by companies based in France, Germany, Italy, Spain and South Korea. On 3 June, in Shenyang, dissident **Guo Chenming**, who was planning a candlelight vigil, sent a message to supporters saying 'an emergency has occurred'. The only public protest allowed anywhere on Chinese territory took place in Hong Kong where an estimated 70,000 people attended the candlelight vigil in Victoria Park. (*Guardian*, Reuters)

The Chinese press avoided any mention of the events of 4 June 1989, although the English-language *China Daily* quoted a foreign ministry spokesman who defended the crackdown. An editorial in the *People's Daily* on 2 June – which argued that the suppression had been 'timely and correct' – was deleted in the English-language version printed by the news agency. Well ahead of the anniversary, the government had taken steps to restrict news. In March, Beijing authorities stopped issuing new publishing licences to newspapers and magazines until the second half of the year. In April, the Hong Kong newspaper *Ming Pao* reported that the communist party committee in Guangdong province had banned all articles about the pro-democracy protests. In May, authorities suspended accreditation of Taiwanese correspondents until after 4 June; companies supplying news to pager owners and computer networks were asked to halt their services temporarily; and cable-operators were told to stop relaying broadcasts by Hong Kong's Phoenix Satellite Television until after 4 June. (*Guardian*, RSF)

In the 10 years since the 1989 crackdown, at least 56 journalists have been imprisoned and five are still in jail: **Yu Dongyue**, an art critic with the *News of Liuyang*, arrested on 23 May 1989 and sentenced to 20 years; **Hu Liping**, a journalist with the *Beijing Daily*, arrested on 7 April 1990 and sentenced to 10 years; **Chen Yambin**, joint editor of the underground

magazine *Tielu*, arrested at the end of 1990 and sentenced to 15 years; **Zhang Yagei**, joint editor of *Tielu*, arrested September 1990 and sentenced to 12 years; and **Liu Jingsheng**, a journalist with the underground magazine *Tansou*, arrested 28 May 1992 and sentenced to 15 years. Journalists who have been released continue to suffer for their support of the democracy movement. **Gao Yu**, a journalist with *Economic Weekly*, was released on 15 February after five and a half years in prison, but is not allowed to leave Beijing or talk to foreign media. Some have been forced to live in exile, and others, such as **Chen Zeming**, are under house arrest. About 20 journalists have been forced to resign, retire or change jobs, and 50 or so have been victims of sanctions. (RSF)

Recent publications: *Growing Media Repression and Self-Restraint in China* (IPI, May 1999, pp 28); *Gross Violations of Human Rights in the Xinjiang Uighur Autonomous Region* (AI, April 1999, pp 92).

COLOMBIA

Journalist **Wilson Lozano** and cameraman **Henry Durn Padilla** of the NTC news agency were attacked in the department of Bolivar on 11 April. The journalists, who suffered minor injuries, were working on a report on the eradication of illegal crops. (IFJ)

Director of the Regional Studies Institute **Professor Hernan Henao Delgado** was assassinated on 4 May while chairing a meeting. Two men and a woman took the professor to a separate room where they shot him three times in the head. (OMCT)

After 15 years, the 'faceless judges' system is due to end on 30 June. Enacted in 1984 during the administration of President Belisario Bentancur, the system was considered a temporary measure that provided anonymity – faces covered and voices distorted – for judges, prosecutors and witnesses in cases of kidnapping, drug trafficking and paramilitary activities. But laws passed in 1988 and 1990 incorporated these judges into the regular courts and the 1991 constitution made the faceless system apparently permanent. (Latin America Press)

CONGO-BRAZZAVILLE

A journalist with pan-African radio station Africa Number One, **Hervé Kiminou-Missou**, was apprehended by the frontier police on 31 May while trying to reach the oil-rich Angolan enclave of Cabinda. Another broadcaster, **Maurice Lemaire**, of the international agency AITV, was also detained. They were held in solitary confinement at a police station in the port of Pointe-Noire. (RSF)

COTE D'IVOIRE

Four journalists from the newspaper Le Populaire have been released, but **Raphael Lakpé**, the editor-in-chief, is still being detained at Abidjan's

Maison d'Arrêt et Correction where he has been held since 28 April. **Idrissa Bamba, Shran Haisy, Junior Mohamed Outtara** and **Yves Abiet** were released on the evening of 3 June. The journalists had been accused of insulting the head of state after writing that he had purchased his doctorate. Lakpé is accused of 'disturbing the public order' and 'distributing false news' after publishing a 28 April article claiming that a student had died during a demonstration in Abidjan when, in fact, he had only been injured. The newspaper had published a correction the following day. (RSF)

CROATIA

On 7 May, the Zagreb public prosecutor indicted **Orlanda Obad**, a journalist from the daily Jutarni List, and four bank workers for revealing and publishing details of President Franjo Tudjman's wife's bank accounts. The publication was deemed to be an infringement of the Tudjmans' privacy and not in the public interest. Jutarni List revealed Ankica Tudjman had deposited nearly DM500,000 (US$275,628) which the president had reportedly failed to declare in a formal statement of his family's assets. (International Press Institute)

CZECH REPUBLIC

On 15 April the Romany Rainbow organisation, representing rent defaulters in the Usti nad Labem town district, agreed with the local council on the construction of a

fence to separate the Roma from houses opposite their apartments. A previous plan to build the wall (Index 4/1998), ostensibly to protect residents from the noise and rubbish created by the Roma, was rejected following human rights protests. (RFE/RL)

DEMOCRATIC REPUBLIC OF CONGO (DRC)

Stephane Kitutu O'Leontwa, president of Congolese Press Union and former president-general of Congolese Radio-Television, was detained on 8 May and placed in solitary confinement until 12 May. O'Leontwa was held instead of a journalist from the Pot Pourri newspaper whom the authorities were seeking in conjunction with three articles that satirised the government, referred to President Laurent Kabila as the 'heir' to former dictator Mobutu Sese Seko, and termed the whole post-independence period as 'wasted years'. (RSF)

EGYPT

On 18 April freelance journalist **Abd al-Munim Gamal al-Din** (Index 4/1998, 5/1998, 2/1999) was acquitted along with 20 other defendants by the supreme military court in the so-called 'Returnees from Albania' trial. He was promptly issued with a new detention order and transferred to Istiqlal prison. (AI))

On 20 April the chief public prosecutor ordered four journalists from Al Shaab newspaper – **Magdy Hussein**,

Adel Hussein, **Salah Bedeiwi** and **Essam Hanafi** – to stand trial on libel charges by Agriculture Minister Yousef Wali. The newspaper accused Wali of harming Egyptian agriculture through his 'overzealous' co-operation with Israeli farming experts. Hussein and another *Al-Shaab* journalist were sentenced in February 1998 to two years in prison although an appeal court subsequently quashed the verdict (*Index* 3/1998, 4/1998, 5/1998, 6/1998). (*Cairo Times*, RSF)

On 2 May public prosecutors ordered the detention of **Hussein Al Matani** on charges of forgery related to his attempts to register a syndicate of independent journalists as a private company. The syndicate was formed last year as an alternative to the official union which controls the accreditation of all journalists. (*Cairo Times*)

On 8 May two journalists, **Hussein Al-Matani** and **Shehata Naguib Ayoub**, were put on trial on charges of publishing eight issues of the independent weekly *Sahebat al-Galala* without a government licence. Al-Mataani is already under investigation for founding the independent journalists' syndicate. (Derechos Human Rights)

The Cabinet of Ministers approved the controversial bill on associations and private institutions which gives the government a veto over how NGOs are organised. It prohibits NGOs from carrying out 'political activities' or any other

that 'threaten national unity or violate public order or moral codes'. It also requires NGO to obtain approval before receiving funds from abroad. (HRW)

Wahba Aboul Ella, a philosophy professor at Minya University's faculty of arts, was joined in a hunger strike by dozens of students to protest the banning of his book *Al Wugoud Al Maqloub* ('The Upside Down Existence'). The book addresses 'Zionist-American influence in the Arab region and the world'. (*Cairo Times*)

ETHIOPIA

On 12 April **Samson Seyum** was sentenced to four and a half years in jail for 'incitement to violence' for certain articles he wrote as editor-in-chief of the Amharic-language weekly *Tequami*. Seyum had been detained since December 1995. (*Index* 1/1999). (RSF)

FIJI

On 21 May the new prime minister, Mahendra Chaudhry, pledged not to legislate against the media or impose licensing and added that his government would look at how best to dispose of the 44 per cent of government shares in the islands' second daily newspaper, the *Daily Post*. (Pacific Islands News Association)

FRANCE

On 9 May the *Journal du Dimanche* newspaper reported that the accidental bombing by NATO of the Chinese embassy

in Belgrade may have actually been planned to stop broadcasts from within by a television channel owned by President Milosevic's daughter. Marija Milosevic is reported to have moved her station, TV Koshva, to the embassy after the headquarters of her father's party was bombed in an earlier NATO raid. (*Daily Telegraph*)

FRENCH POLYNESIA

On 17 April French Polynesian President Gaston Flosse lifted a seven-year-old ban on the pro-independence radio station Te Reo o Tefana and pledged to open up news conferences to all news media in Tahiti for the first time since 1992. The station had challenged a ban President Flosse had imposed on their attendance at his press conferences. (Pacific Media Watch)

GEORGIA

On 27 and 28 April Interfax reported claims that officials in southern Georgia had seized six tonnes of religious material produced by the Jehovah's Witnesses and arrested the Turkish driver of the lorry transporting the cargo. The reports said that the 20 million religious tracts and video cassettes were of high quality, but did not specify the language. (RFE/RL)

GUATEMALA

Military 'death squads' kept detailed records of their operations, according to a document released by four human rights organisations and public interest groups on 20 May. The 54-page document – the only one of its kind to be revealed – contains photos and names of 183 students, union leaders, professors, doctors and housewives arrested between 1983 and 1985 in and around Guatemala City: over 100 of them were killed. Some were arrested simply for having once travelled to Cuba. The document was bought for US$2,000 from a former officer, who smuggled it out of army intelligence files and handed it to human rights advocates in February. The log-book covers death squad activity by intelligence units during an 18-month period from August 1983 to March 1985. Retired Gen. Oscar Humberto Mejia Victores, who ruled from 1983 to 1986, has denied allegations of army involvement in the disappearance, torture and execution of guerrilla sympathisers. 'Such a counter-insurgency unit never existed. Those accusations are politically motivated and come from those who wanted to set up a communist regime in Guatemala.' (American National Security Archive, *La Nacion*, HRW, Reuters)

In response to the 25 February publication of the Historical Clarification Commission's report into the country's civil war, former president Vinicio Cerezo (1986-91) has said that the US government knew about the extrajudicial executions carried out by army death squads and that they prevented him from revealing the facts while he was in office. During his March

trip to the country, President Clinton made a limited apology for the US role in the civil war saying that officials should have steered clear of military units that 'engaged in violence and widespread repression'. (*La Nacion*, HRW)

Bruce Harris, executive director of the children's rights NGO Casa Alianza, suffered a defeat in a defamation case against him when the decision that his case could be heard by a Printer's Tribunal was overturned. The decision means Harris's case will now be heard in a criminal court. The case was brought by Susana de Umana, wife of the ex-President of the Supreme Court and has been passed from court to court over the past 18 months. In 1997, Harris alleged that Susana de Umana was among a number of lawyers who used undue influence and illegal practices to process international adoptions of Guatemalan children. De Umana accused Harris of defamation, slander and injury. (Casa Alianza)

GHANA

An Accra high court ordered the *Ghanaian Chronicle* to pay an unprecedented fine of 42 million cedis (US$835) for libel against Edward Salia, Minister of Roads and Transport. It follows an article in the *Chronicle* entitled 'Vetting begins, Minister in a bribery scandal' which alleged that Salia had requested US$25,000 from Milicom Ghana, a cellphone operator. (Free Expression Ghana)

GREECE

On 19 May **Charalambos Triantafyllidis**, editor and publisher of the weekly *Enimerosi* in Florina, northwest Greece, was given a five-month suspended sentence for insulting Florina's then prefect-elect, Pavlos Altanis. The editorial, it was claimed, was no more than strong criticism. Triantafyllidis was also fined Dr500,000 (US$1,635) for damages. (Greek Helsinki Monitor)

On 21 May the editor and publisher of the daily *Adesmeftos Typos*, **Dimitris Rizos**, was convicted by an Athens court and sentenced to 12 months in prison for the repeated defamation of four members of the board of directors of rival daily *Eleftheros Typos*. Rizos, who accused the four of embezzlement in a 1944 television interview, had his sentence changed to a fine and, after payment, he was set free. (Greek Helsinki Monitor)

GUINEA

Jean-Baptiste Kourama, associate editor-in-chief of the weekly *L'Independent Plus*, was arrested on 26 April following the publication of two articles accusing two state officials of taking bribes. (RSF)

INDIA

On 2 June Minister for Information Pramod Mahajan banned the transmission of Pakistan television (PTV) by cable operators because of the 'vilification campaign against India, especially in connection with the Kargil situation,' a reference to operations recently launched by the Indian army in Kashmir. All independent international media were banned in Indian-ocupied Kashmir, in efforts to maintain an almost complete news blackout. (Agence France Presse, Pakistan Press Foundation)

Recent Publication: *The Enron Corporation: Corporate Complicity in Human Rights Violations* (Human Rights Watch, January 1999, pp 163).

INDONESIA

On 12 April one English and two Australian journalists escaped serious injury when the motorcade of Timorese leader Bishop Carlos Belo was attacked by members of the Red and White Iron militia while driving through Liquicia. The previous week, at least 25 people were allegedly killed in Liquicia in an massacre by pro-Indonesian militia. The Bishop's car was not attacked, but the motorcade was chased out of the village. (Pacific Media Watch)

Four directors of East Timor's most popular television station, RCTI, quit their jobs on 17 May, the same day that coverage of the election campaign period was scheduled to begin. RCTI's president **Ralie Siregar**, with the station for nine years, and his deputy **Alex Kumara**, said they left willingly. 'We just want to give opportunities to other people to manage this private network,' said Siregar, 'There

was no political intervention.' Marketing director **R Hardiyanto** and financial director **Ishar Baharuddin** also resigned. (Pacific Media Watch)

On 24 May the Australian ambassador asked embassy officials in Jakarta to seek assurances for the safety of *Sydney Morning Herald* correspondent **Mark Dodd** and photographer **Jason South**, after a group opposing East Timor independence accused the men of bias and declared: 'Blackmailers should be stopped'. The group which made the threats, the Forum for Unity, Democracy and Justice, is linked to pro-Jakarta paramilitary groups. The request follows weeks of threats against journalists. On 10 May, Canadian journalist **Ian Timberlake** was attacked in a Dili taxi by militiamen wielding home-made weapons. President Habibie ruled out any special protection for journalists. 'It's against your own idea of press freedom,' he told the *Herald*. 'If you think it's not worthwhile to come, then don't come.' (Pacific Media Watch, Pacific Islands News Association)

IRAN

On 21 April **Mohsen Kadivar**, a reformist Islamic scholar and professor of philosophy, was sentenced to 18 months' imprisonment by the Special Court for the Clergy (*Index* 3/1999). It is thought that the charges are related to Kadivar's 14 February article in the *Khordad* newspaper, his university lectures and a series of

essays in which he argued that politics and religion should be separated. (*Al-Quds al-'Arabi*, WiPC, PEN)

Azeri journalist **Qanimat Zahidov**, editor-in-chief of the Baku-based daily *Ekspress Gazeta*, disappeared on 3 May. According to staff, Zahidov had conducted an interview with dissident university professor **Mahmudali Johragani**, a professor at Tabriz University who is known to support the rights of the Azeri minority. According to sources, the authorities ignored all inquiries from Baku before finally releasing him on 30 May. Zahidov later alleged that the National Security Ministry had attempted to recruit him as a spy. (Human Rights Center of Azerbaijan, RFE/RL, (CPJ)

Fereydoun Verdinejad, director of the state news agency IRNA and publisher of the Iran Press Group, was arrested on 29 May and held for six hours before being released on the payment of 180 million rial (US$60,000). Verdinejad is a known reformist. (RSF)

On 29 May the publisher of the reformist daily *Arya*, **Mohammed Reza Zohdi**, was sent to jail on charges of 'publishing slanderous material, disturbing public opinion and exposing military secrets.' He was unable to meet the 210 million rial (US$70,000) bail. (RSF)

ISRAEL

It was reported on 19 April that

136   INDEX ON CENSORSHIP 4 1999

● ●

FA'EZEH HASHEMI
Why Zan?

I have turned into a counter-revolutionary and monarchist overnight! The pretext is a cartoon and a news item in the 3 April 1999 issue of *Zan* newspaper. Why did they give rise to such a commotion?

Recent events have shown that 'extensive reaction' has begun – and in the garb of *shari'ah* and the law at that. This reaction is composed of different elements. Most prominent is the provision of wrong information to hide who the real enemy is. While an offspring of the revolution is described as an enemy, an evil hand emerged from its sleeve to slay Lt-Gen Sayyad-Shirazi [an Iranian commander assassinated in April].

When it is announced in a newspaper that 'the US is secretly running affairs in [the press] from behind the scenes', the focus strays to imaginary enemies, so that the real enemy can carry out its conspiracies at leisure. Tyranny can only succeed if there is a split in the ranks of freedom-loving Muslims. If they abandon moderation, which is their vital force, and give into violence, it can turn rapidly to chaos, from the heart of which a coup can be concocted.

The most cunning propaganda, which is tyrannical in content and Islamic in appearance, is to describe the children of the revolution as 'monarchists'. When a person like myself is labelled a monarchist! How is this to be interpreted? This is the most subtle ploy resorted to by 'hidden hands'.

A free and prospering Iran under Islam, in the heart of the strategic Middle East, could be a spark that sets the whole area alight without the need for slogans or physical action. Iranian women stand at the forefront as always. The attacks against me and *Zan* by men whose views about women are well known, are intended to break that front.

I, Fa'ezeh Hashimi, a Muslim, an Iranian and an Iranian woman, with a *chador* over my head, a pen in my hand and a life ready to be offered for sacrifice, wish to see an Iran that is Islamic, free and devoid of tyranny; and Iran for all Iranians. And I will not abandon the trench of freedom. ❏

Fa'ezeh Hashimi, daughter of former president Akbar Hashimi Rafsanjani and a principal supporter of President Mohammed Khatami's glasnost programme, is editor of Zan, Iran's first woman's magazine. In early April, Zan was banned indefinitely for running an interview with the widow of the former Shah of Iran and publishing a cartoon satirising Islamic laws on women.
Translated by Nilou Mobasser

● ●

Qassem Dargham, a cameraman for Abu Dhabi TV, was shot in the back by troops near Arnoun following the extension of Israel's Southern Lebanon occupation zone. Eleven journalists present at the scene said that they were deliberately targeted by the occupying troops. In 1998 11 journalists were reportedly shot by Israeli soldiers and a further 23 were beaten either by troops or Jewish settlers. (RSF)

On 27 May armed forces violently attacked a peaceful demonstration in Israeli-occupied East Jerusalem, injuring eight journalists: **Rulal Al Halawani** (Reuters), **Awad Awad** (AFP), **Mahfouz Abu Turk** (Reuters), **Ishaq Al Qawasmi** (Orient House photographer), **Atta Iweisat** (Zoom 77 Agency), **Moussa Armoun** (France 2), **Khaled Jahshan** (PBC) and **Shorouq Al Asa'ad**. (OMCT)

JAPAN

On 18 May the country's first freedom of information law was passed into law, 20 years after the first proposed bill was drafted by the Japan Civil Liberties Union. The new law is weaker than that sought by reformers, allowing the goverment considerable scope to withhold information deemed damaging to national security interests or foreign relations, as well as preventing the disclosure of trade secrets. In a provision which, it is claimed, goes further than US law, however, information that has a direct bearing on public health or safety must be released,

whether or not its disclosure would infringe privacy, property or corporate secrecy rights. (*International Herald Tribune*)

A law banning the purchase of sex from anyone 17 or younger was approved unanimously by the Lower House on 18 May. The new law also bans the manufacture, sale and distribution of obscene photographs, videos and Internet images of children. It is estimated that four-fifths of the world's child pornography is produced in Japan. (*Economist, Japan Times*)

On 1 June, the Lower House approved a package of bills that will allow wiretapping of private communications in investigations of organised crime. The bills passed without much public debate. (*Japan Times*)

KAZAKSTAN

Opposition leaders **Seydakhmet Quttyqadam** and **Amirzhan Qosanov** told a 27 April Almaty press conference that the proposed media law before Parliament was 'very far from democratic' and 'would increase state control over all periodicals, television channels and radio stations.' (RFE/RL, Interfax)

Journalist **Armial Tasymbekov**, accused of painting slogans on buildings and fences in Astana that denounced President Nursultan Nazarbaev and lauded former Premier Akezhan Kazhegeldin (*Index* 3/1999), was arrested by National Security Committee

officials on his arrival at Almaty main station from Astana on 30 April and taken to a psychiatric clinic. Tasymbekov told a journalist who managed to meet him in the clinic on 3 May that he had been interrogated about the graffiti by a National Security Committee colonel. Tasymbekov was released on 5 May. A doctor at the clinic said the journalist had been treated for 'a temporary mental disorder' which he was 'forbidden by law' from revealing, but that he was now 'absolutely sober and healthy'. (RFE/RL)

An Almaty district court opened hearings on 5 May in a case brought by former Premier Akezhan Kazhegeldin against the justice ministry for refusing to register the *Respublika* newspaper, which is published by Kazhegeldin's Republican People's Party of Kazakstan. Amirzhan Qosanov, a member of the party's executive board, told journalists that all the necessary documents for the official registration of *Respublika* were submitted to the Justice Ministry in August 1998. (RFE/RL)

KENYA

The officer commanding Karatina police station on 20 May threatened to 'teach' **Stephen Munyiri** a 'lesson' over a news report he filed for the *Daily Nation*. The officer alleged that the journalist had tarnished his name over a report that two children aged four and six were held at the police station together with their father. (*Daily Nation*)

Two journalists, **Robert Wafula** of the *Daily Nation* and his *East African Standard* counterpart **John Muganda**, are set to sue Bungoma district administrator Ibrahim Duale for ridiculing them in public. The government administrator had told a public rally that the two journalists were '*chang'aa* (a banned spirit) drinkers and bribe-takers'. The administrator was ostensibly unhappy with their reporting and offered to preside over a funds drive for them, saying they were poorly paid. (*Daily Nation*)

Recent publication: Steeves, H. Leslie, 1998: *Gender Violence and the Press: The St Kizito Story* Ohio University Press. 176 pages. Price $17.95; Throup David, 1998: *Multi-party Politics in Kenya: The Kenyatta and Moi States and the Triumph of the System in the 1992 Election* Ohio University Press. 290 pages. Price $29.95

An intruder erased computer files relating to former KGB members at the weekly newspaper *Asaba* during the night of 24 to 25 April. Although there was no sign of forced entry and nothing was stolen, password-protected archive files on employees of the National Security Ministry (the KGB's successor) had been deleted. The raid came two days after a call to the newspaper from the deputy national security minister demanding the surrender of documents containing 'negative information' on his employees

and threatening prosecution if the information were published. Asaba was evicted from its former offices on 18 August 1998 (*Index* 6/1998). (RFE/RL)

On 1 May Bishkek City Court confirmed a 200,000 sum (US$6,670) fine levied on the independent weekly *Res Publika* a month earlier for insulting the 'honour and dignity' of Amanbek Karypkulov, president of Kyrgyzstan's National Television and Radio Corporation (*Index* 3/1999). On 12 January the newspaper published an open letter from 20 employees at the corporation to President Askar Akaev and other officials protesting that Karypkulov had repressed media freedom since the early 1980s. Editor **Yuri Maksimov** is to appeal to the Supreme Court. (RFE/RL)

On 6 May Limby Maharavo, head of the minister of culture and information's cabinet, gave an order banning **James Ramarosaona**, president of the Madagascar Order of Journalists, from appearing on public television (TVM). Ramarosaona had been invited by **Johary Ravoajanahary**, a leading TVM journalist, to debate the theme of journalists' freedoms on the weekly *Varo-Jabo* programme. The ban was issued the day after celebrations marking World Press Freedom Day. (IFJ)

On 12 May the trial began of journalist **Maka Alphonse** for having distributed false

information concerning Minister of Health Henriette Rahantalalao. (IFJ)

On 18 May 1999, the High Court ordered the country's Electoral Commission to ensure that the state-controlled Malawi Broadcasting Corporation (MBC) provide fair coverage to all political players in the run-up to the general elections. The case arose when three private citizens, **Charles Kafumba**, **Luke Banda** and **Laurent Kamulette**, sued the commission and the corporation when the latter continued to give President Bakili Muluzi and his ruling United Democratic Front party full access to the radio at the expense of other presidential aspirants. In his ruling, Justice Mackson Mkandawire instructed that the commission 'be directed to take concrete steps to ensure that all competitors in the electoral process have equal and/or fair access to all state-controlled media'. (Media Institute of South Africa)

Daily Times sports reporter **Pilirani Kachinziri** was assaulted on 22 May by a Telcom Wanderers Football team fan for allegedly writing negative stories about Wanderers official Jack Kamwendo and national team coach Jack Chamangwana. A report in the *Daily Times* said that Kachinziri was attacked at half-time during the Cosafa Castle Cup match between Malawi and Namibia. (MISA)

A High Court injunction on 24

May restrained the pro-opposition Malawi Congress Party newspaper *National Agenda* from writing articles about the deputy campaign director for the United Democratic Front (UDF) Mary Nyandovi-Kerr and her husband David Kerr. The paper had alleged an extra-marital affair by Kerr. (MISA)

MALAYSIA

A far-reaching gagging order had been issued by Judge Abdul Wahab Patel barring news organisations from publishing anything but 'factual evidence' during the imminent sodomy trial of dismissed deputy prime minister Anwar Ibrahim. The trial, which began on 7 June, charges Ibrahim with 'carnal intercourse against the order of nature'. (*International Herald Tribune*, *Guardian*, Associated Press)

MAURITANIA

On 9 April the French and Arab language editions of *Le Calame* were banned for three months by order of the ministry of the interior. The newspaper was suspended on three separate occasions in 1998 (*Index 2/1998, 4/1998*). (RSF)

Cheikh Bekaye, a correspondent in Nouakchott with the BBC since 1986 and the London-based, Arab-language daily *El Hayat* since 1989, had his accreditation revoked by the ministry of communications on 15 April. No reason was given. (RSF)

MEXICO

On 26 May in Guadalajara army intelligence colonel **Pedro Castellanos** was convicted of breaching army discipline and abuse of office but found not guilty of the more serious charge that he fed military secrets to the national weekly news magazine *Proceso*. Castellanos was arrested in April 1997 after *Proceso* published an article on links between the army and drug trafficking. He pleaded not guilty and *Proceso* journalists said Castellanos was not their source. (Reuters)

On 8 April **Carina Ochoa**, journalist with the independent magazine *La Guillotina*, was on her way home by subway when an unknown man sat in front of her and started asking her questions about her work. He then threatened her and her colleagues, saying: 'You should take care otherwise you are dead meat, and tell your colleagues to lie low, or to keep quiet or something might happen to them.' On the same day, **Fabiola Espinosa Fuentes**, sister of a member of the editorial board of the magazine, received a threatening phone call. *La Guillotina* has given widespread coverage to the conflict in Chiapas, as well as the EZLN. On 15 March two employees who filmed a public debate between the inhabitants of Atlzapán and Zapatista delegates were intercepted by gunmen, who violently removed their video camera. Over the last few weeks, the editors have received threatening phone calls. Such

incidents have been reported to the authorities, but they do not appear to have been investigated. (AI, OMCT)

On the morning of the 4 May, **Jesús Barraza**, formerly editor of *La Prensa* but now editor of the weekly magazine *Pulso* in San Luis Río Colorado, was leaving the offices of the paper when he was approached by a stranger and offered money not to publish any stories concerning Albino Quintero Meraz, a reputed drug trafficker. If Barraza refused the offer, he was warned, he or another *Pulso* reporter would be killed. The paper had published two articles which reported alleged cooperation between Quintero and former Quintana Roo state governor Mario Villanueva, who is wanted in connection with drugs trafficking. Police protection has been granted to Barraza, yet fears persist for his safety. (CPJ)

Recent Publications: *José Martí Reader: Writings on the Americas* (1999, 300pp); *For La Partia: Politics and the Armed Forces in Latin America* (Brian Loveman 1999, 424pp); *Mexico's Hope: An Encounter With Politics and History* (James Cockcroft 1999, 320pp); *Subnational Politics and Democratization in Mexico* (Cornelius, Eisenstadt & Hindley 1999, 365pp).

MONGOLIA

Crime reporter **L. Munkhbayasgalan**, of the weekly *Seruulag* (Alarm Clock), was seriously injured by unknown men in a razor attack on 6 April which left her with deep cuts to her face, hands and neck. The attack followed a letter and calls the previous week threatening that she would 'be a pretty girl that no one can look at', or 'become a corpse.' Munkhbayasgalan had been covering the trial of former Conservative Party leader O. Dashbalbar, who is accused of the attempted rape of another *Seruulag* journalist. (RSF)

MOZAMBIQUE

A court in Cabo Delgado sentenced Severino Charles, a local police commander, to six months imprisonment for the illegal detention of journalist **Fernando Quionova** (*Index* 3/1999) in December 1998. However Charles was granted the option to pay a fine of 546,000 meticais (US$44) plus damages to Quionova of 3 million meticais (US$240). President Mocumbi denounced the crime as an act of press censorship and encouraged reporters to expose others. (RSF)

NEPAL

Krishna Sen, editor of the Nepali-language weekly *Janadesh*, **Dhana Bahadur Magar**, the paper's office manager, and **Sher Bahadur Basnet**, a press assistant, were arrested on 20 April and thousands of copies of that week's issue were seized. All three have yet to be formally charged, but their arrests were apparently in connection with his paper's publication that week of an interview with Babaram

Bhattarai, one of the leaders of the country's Maoist insurgency. (CPJ, RSF)

NIGERIA

On 7 April **Tunde Sanni**, correspondent of the *Post Express* newspaper, and **Kayode Abdulwahab**, correspondent of *This Day* newspaper, were beaten by soldiers attached to the house of the late Gen. Tunde Idiagbon while waiting to meet president-elect General Olusegun Obsanjo. Six other waiting journalists were driven away. (RSF, Nigeria Media Monitor)

Alhaja Bolade Fasasi, a female journalist and treasurer of the Lagos State Council of the National Union of Journalists (NUJ), was shot dead by unknown gunmen in Ibadan on 7 April. On 25 April **Lanre Arogundade**, NUJ chairman and a well-known activist, was charged with Fasasi's murder after police received a petition for his apprehension from two other NUJ members, Lawrence Ojabo and Adeyeye Oyedokun. Arogundade was arraigned by a magistrates court on 4 May, though they do not have the power to try murder cases. Observers are concerned because similar tactics were used against **Ken Saro Wiwa** and the Ogoni 21. Bail was granted on 14 May. (RSF, Nigeria Media Monitor)

Freelance journalist **Fidelis Ikwuebe** was abducted and killed on 18 April during inter-communal clashes in Aguleri. Similarly **Sam Nimfa-Jan** of

Details magazine was killed in Plateau State during clashes between the Hausa-Fulani and the Zangon-Kataf tribes. (RSF)

On 1 May **John Oseze-Langley**, editor of the *Weekend Diet*, was arrested by plain-clothes members of the anti-fraud squad following the publication of an article entitled 'Why Commasie Retired'. Oseze-Langley was released after three hours. (Nigeria Media Monitor)

PAKISTAN

On 14 April international concern was raised about the safety of **Asma Jehangir**, the UN Special Rapporteur on Extra-judicial Killings, and human rights defender **Hina Jilani**. The two activists were recently threatened with death for their defence of **Samia Sarwar**, who had been trying to obtain a divorce. The threats were issued by the extreme conservative *Jamiat-e-Ulema-e-Islam* party and other religious groups and have been backed by members of the Peshawar Chamber of Commerce. The threats follow upon the 'honour killing' of Sarwar by her family. (HRW)

In mid-April journalists **Shamsul Haq** and **Rana Jaffar Hussein** were arrested by police in Muridke, Punjab province, and detained under the Maintenance of Public Order law. Both claim that they were arrested under false pretences because they have reported on the misdeeds of the police. (Pakistan Press Foundation)

• •

NAJAM SETHI

On the eve of the new millenium

The question remains: how do Pakistanis get out of this hell? First, what sort of agendas are required to get out of this hell? Second, who will implement such agendas? I ask my fellow Pakistanis to look at each of the crises referred to above and I demand that the factors which have led to the crisis should be swiftly addressed.

a) Crisis of ideology: There is only one modern-day ideology which will be acceptable to all, irrespective of caste, creed, gender, region, ethnicity, sect, etc. It is the ideology of economic growth, full employment, distributive justice and social welfare.

b) Crisis of law, Constitution and political system: Pakistan must revise the Constitution so that [it and] the political system are made to serve the people below, instead of the corrupt elites above.

c) Crisis of economy: Pakistan should honour its international contracts; tax the rich; dispossess the corrupt; live within its means; vitalise its human resources; export the value of its scientific talents; establish and enforce a genuine private–public partnership.

d) Crisis of civil society: I say, enforce the rule of law; disarm society; disband militias; decentralise decision-making; establish accountability; protect minorities and women; create social nets for the disadvantaged, poor and destitute; provide decentralised and quick justice.

e) Crisis of foreign policy: I say make friends, not masters or enemies; bury Cold-War hatchets; renounce post-Cold-War *jihads*; negotiate terms of trade, not territorial ambitions; redefine strategic depth to mean emphasis on internal will, rather than external space;

f) Crisis of national security: I say redefine security to mean not only military defence but economic vitality, social cohesion and international respect; and I say Pakistan should determine its minimal optimal defence deterrent, but shun an arms race.

The answer to the second question – namely, who will pursue and implement this agenda – is difficult: I cannot see even one leader or institution [with] the three elements needed to get us out of this mess: the vision to chart a particular course; the courage to implement it ruthlessly; and the integrity to ensure it doesn't get derailed. ❏

*An excerpt from a speech delivered by journalist **Najam Sethi** to the India-Pakistan Friendship Society on 20 April in Dehli, for which he was later arrested by Pakistan's Inter-Service Intelligence agency.*

• •

Mehmood Ali Khan Lodhi, a journalist working for the *News* and the government-controlled Associated Press of Pakistan (APP), was picked up by intelligence agents in Lahore on 1 May and interrogated for two days before being released. According to Lhodi, his interrogators wanted to know the details of his involvement with a BBC crew producing a documentary on corruption allegations involving Prime Minister Nawaz Sharif's family business. Lhodi added that he had received death threats while cooperating with the BBC. (Pakistan Press Foundation)

Following his interviews with a BBC team investigating corruption, **Hussain Haqqani**, a regular columnist for the *Friday Times* and the Urdu-language daily *Jang*, was kidnapped on 4 May by a group of agents from Pakistan's Federal Investigation Agency (FIA). Subsequently, a Lahore High Court judge ordered the provincial government to respond to a *habeas corpus* petition by Haqqani's lawyer. Limited access to Haqqani was then allowed, but his lawyer was only able to meet him in the presence of FIA staff. Then, in late May, after alleging that Haqqani had been tortured while in custody, Haqqani's lawyer was again denied access to him. According to reports, Haqqani is being held on a two-year-old corruption charge that is no longer valid. (AI, CPJ)

On 5 May **Ejaz Haider**, an editor with the weekly *Friday Times*, received an anonymous letter advising him to 'drape the windows of [his] car with flak-jackets'. Haider believes that this intimidation is linked to his collaboration with his colleague **Najam Sethi**. The same day, the car of **Imtiaz Alam**, a journalist with the *News*, was burned in front of his house by a group of unidentified men. (RSF)

Najam Sethi, founder and editor-in-chief of the English-language weekly *Friday Times*, was arrested by members of the Inter-Services Intelligence (ISI) on 8 May. Government officials, including Information Minister Mushahid Hussain, claim that Sethi's arrest was linked to an allegedly 'anti-Pakistan' speech he gave to the India-Pakistan Friendship Society in New Delhi on problems facing the country. Sethi's colleagues, on the other hand, argue that his arrest is an attempt by the government to strengthen its recent crackdown on journalists critical of its activities, particularly those who cooperated with a BBC team investigating claims of government corruption. (AI, CPJ, RSF, *Guardian*, BBC World Service, Pakistan Press Foundation)

On 13 May issues of the *Friday Times* were illegally confiscated by authorities in Lahore, just as they were about to be taken to other cities. (AI)

On 19 May Lahore police assaulted **Naseer Chaudry**, a photographer for the evening newspaper *Naya Akhabar*, and **Zahid Ali Khan**, a reporter for the daily *Khabrain*. The journalists had been covering a funeral procession for four alleged robbers who were killed in a police encounter. (Pakistan Press Foundation)

In late May the Punjab government cancelled the publication licence of the quarterly newsletter of the Human Rights Commission of Pakistan (HRCP) because the organisation had not informed the provincial government's information department of its change of address and printer. Nor did it send the department two copies of the newsletter, as required under the terms of the licence. (Pakistan Press Foundation)

On 26 May it was reported that 4,000 copies of the London weekly *Economist* were seized without explanation at Karachi Airport. The lead story of the Asia edition was headlined 'The rot in Pakistan' and focused on Prime Minister Sharif's recent crackdown on press freedom. (RSF)

According to the 1 June issue of the daily *Frontier Post*, 'the federal government has decided to establish a special media cell comprising officials from the police, the Intelligence Bureau and the Federal Investigaton Agency to punish independent journalists critical of government policies'. The report went on to say that 'the *modus operandi* of the special cell would be to abduct a "defiant" journalist and subject him to physical torture at some "safe houses" and release him after 24 or 36 hours'. So far, the newspaper has not received any reaction to its report from the central government. (RSF)

After three weeks of local and international protests on behalf of detained journalist **Najam Sethi** – during which the Inter Services Intelligence (ISI) was accused of torturing him and a legal appeal had to be taken to the Supreme Court before Sethi was allowed access to his family and lawyer – he was released without charge on 2 June. Subsequently, the Supreme Court said that it would decide on the legality of Sethi's arrest by the ISI after the summer vacations. (AI, CPJ, RSF, *Guardian*, BBC World Service, Pakistan Press Foundation)

Recent Publication: *Pakistan: Juveniles sentenced to death* (AI, May 1999).

PALESTINE (AUTONOMOUS AREAS)

On 26 April Palestinian security forces in Hebron verbally ordered Amal TV to suspend broadcasting for allegedly jamming the frequencies of the official Palestine TV. Amal TV journalists claimed to be unaware of any such jamming attempts and suspected instead that the closure was in reprisal for a programme about corruption in Islam or about the broadcast story of a man who had held his son captive in a cave in Hebron. The station was allowed to resume service in mid-May. (CPJ)

On 17 May the authorities' Preventive Security Services

(PSS) ordered Bethlehem-based Al-Rao' TV to suspend broadcasting following a 13 May broadcast of a play, *Natrin Faraj*, which the authorities claimed incited 'prejudice' between Christians and Muslims. Staff reported that an official closure order was handed to them by PSS Chief Jabril Rajoub on 19 May. Al-Roa' ('Shepherd') TV has been the target of official harassment for over a year (*Index* 3/1998, 2/1999), most recently in late April 1999 when official Palestine TV took over its more powerful distribution frequencies at a cost to Al-Roa' of US$17,000. (CPJ)

On 22-23 May security authorities arrested three journalists working for the *Al-Risala* ('The Message'), newspaper of the Islamic Al-Khalas Party in Gaza, in response to the 20 May publication of an article concerning the alleged torture of prisoner Ayman Amassi. The article contained accounts by Amassi's family of the torture which contradicted the official view that Amassi had attempted to hang himself while in custody. According to the medical reports released by the Al-Shifa hospital, where Amassi is now held, Amassi's upper arms are blue from apparent blows and there are red marks around his neck. Managing editor **Ghazi Hamad** was released on the night of 23 May having been ordered not to publish any further information about Amassi. However, editor **Wisam Efeefa** and editor-in-chief **Mahmoud al-Bardaweel**, who wrote the article, remain in detention. (CPJ)

PERU

Judge Julia Eguia Davalos denounced on 12 April irregularities in the investigation of the kidnapping of journalist **Pedro Yauri Bustamante**, whose file was returned without proper investigation by the Public Ministry Executive Committee. The judge has asked for the inquiry to be reopened and proposed assigning another attorney to the case. Bustamante was kidnapped on 24 June 1992. (IFJ)

On 14 April the director of the Huaraz newspaper *YA*, **Pedro Maguina Calderón**, denounced an attack on the newspaper's premises. Two people broke down the doors and interrupted the edition for over an hour, after which they threatened the family of a journalist who lived in the same building. The police were able to capture the assailants, employees of the local hydroelectric plant owned by the company, Egenor. *YA* had criticised the safety of the plant on repeated occasions. (IFJ)

On 21 April journalist **Fernando Santos Rojas** received death threats (*Index* 1/1999) while working on his radio programme *Libertad de Prensa* (Press Freedom) on Satipo radio. The threats came from relatives of Mayor Miguel Durand, whom Rojas had accused of corruption. In a previous radio interview, Durand assaulted the journalist on air while making gestures which indicated his throat would be cut. A couple of days before, a group of 15 people broke into the radio station to threaten Santos Rojas. (Instituto di Prensa Y Sociedad, IFJ)

On 4 May magistrates Eduardo Macedo Zapata and assistant Jose Manuel Monteverde Tuesta were dismissed from their posts in relation to the investigation into the assassination of journalist **Tito Pilco Mori** (*Index* 3/1999). On 22 April the Chief Prosecutor had accepted an appeal by Tito Pilco's widow against a previous resolution to terminate the investigation of the murder. The decision was taken in the light of an Ombudsman's report which contained a cassette recording of an interview giving explicit details of the preparation of the crime. Tito Pilco, director and owner of Radio Frecuencia Popular in Rioja, died on 3 September 1997 after being attacked by six men. (RSF)

On 24 April **Estela Alejos Alejos**, a correspondent in Sihuas province, was verbally abused by the mayor of the locality and expelled from a public meeting. Alejos, a victim of violent attacks because of her critical views on municipal management, was trying to gather information on cattle rustling. Last year she had another clash with the mayor when trying to interview him during the electoral campaign. Alejos is editor of *Chasqui* magazine and works as a correspondent for *La Industria de Chimbote* and *Prensa Regional de Huaraz*. (Instituto di Prensa Y Sociedad)

On 29 April Radio Espacial reporter **Miguel Gutierrez Cipriano** was assaulted and threatened with death by two unknown people. Gutierrez had reported on the results of an audit of the Otuzco municipality which clearly showed misappropriation of public funds. (Instituto di Prensa Y Sociedad)

On 29 April businessman **Baruch Ivcher** ((*Index* 4/1997, 5/1997, 6/1997, 2/1998, 3/1998, 4/1998, 5/1998, 6/1998, 1/1999, 2/1999) made public official confidential documents revealing a governmental plan to attack the press and prosecute journalists. The documents were addressed to the director of the army intelligence and ordered a 24-hour surveillance of critical journalists. According to Ivcher the dailies *El Comercio* and *La República* were particularly targeted by the plan. (Instituto di Prensa Y Sociedad)

Reporter **Agripino Figueroa** and photo-journalist **Armando Sanchez**, of the newspapers *La Voz de los Andes* and *El Cono Norte* respectively, were detained by the police on 4 May. They were covering a confrontation between municipal officers and street vendors when the police approached them and took their cameras away. (Instituto di Prensa Y Sociedad)

On 18 May the Piura Criminal Court began to consider the assassination of journalists **Isabel Chumpitaz Panta** and **José Amaya Jacinto** (*Index* 3/1998, 4/1998). The motive for the

killing has not been resolved and only nine of the 16 assailants who broke into Chumpitaz's house have been detained, though a warrant exists for the detention of the other seven. (IFJ)

On 31 May the magazine *Repúdica* was launched with the logo of the daily *La República* newspaper, under a false editor's name and giving no contact details. The 16-page, colour publication will appear three times per week and appears to be connected with local tabloids, *Mananero* and *Chuchi*, both of which have been implicated in a slander campaign against *La República*'s director, **Gustavo Mohme Llona** (*Index* 1/1999, 4/1998). Since 31 March Mohme has also been targeted by the daily *El Tio* which has published at least 10, full-page articles insulting Mohme. In June 1998, journalists held a demonstration against the three papers, all of which have ties with the government. The campaign has so far targeted journalists and politicians such as **Cesar Hildebrandt** (*Index* 2/1998, 4/1998), **Angel Paez** (*Index* 4/1998, 5/1998) , **Edmundo Cruz** (*Index* 4/1998), **José Arrieta** (*Index* 2/1998, 3/1998, 4/1998), **Cecilia Valenzuela** (*Index* 4/1998) and **Fernando Rosgipliosan**. The legal representative of the Association for the Defence of the Truth (APRODEV) Hector Ricardo Faisal Fracalossi has been accused with being responsible for the campaign, having used APRODEV's web site for the same purpose. Faisal has failed to turn up to answer such charges in court on several occasions. (Instituto di Prensa Y Sociedad)

On 31 May **Antonio Llerena Marotti**, journalist and opposition member of congress, was sacked from the radio station El Sol where he has worked for 28 years and 10 months. He claimed that there was a political motive behind the closure of his programme which broadcast harsh criticism of the Fujimori government. 'Once more, the public has been informed that freedom of the press does not exist in the country, nor are media outlets which tell the truth and denounce irregularities wanted,' said Llarena Marotti. (IFJ)

PHILIPPINES

Four senior journalists have resigned from the *Manila Times* in protest at an apology by the newspaper's publisher, Robina Gokongwei-Pe, to President Joseph Estrada in a bid to halt a 101m peso (US$2.6m) libel case brought against it by the adminstration. Managing editor **Chit Estella**, associate editor **Booma Cruz**, chief reporter **Eduardo Lingao** and chief business reporter **Joel Gaborni** said the act was an expression of their concern that the newspaper's independence and integrity were being sacrificed to appease the government. The lawsuit, filed on 9 March, was the administration's response to an article which reported that, by witnessing a signing ceremony to close a deal between the government-run National Power Corporation

and the Argentine firm IMPSA Asia Ltd, Estrada has become an 'unwitting *ninong* (godfather)' to the allegedly improper contract. Estrada withdrew his suit on 8 May, following a front-page apology. (CPJ)

RUSSIA

On 15 April **Ruben Arutiunian**, a journalist for the human rights weekly *Express Chronicle*, was sentenced to 10 days' imprisonment for hooliganism, following a 10-minute court session witnessed by only the police officers who had beaten him up the previous day. The officers had stopped Arutiunian on 14 April while he was taking photographs for a report on the criminal justice system. (RSF)

Altaf Galeev, director of Titan independent radio station in Ufa city, Bashkortostan, was released from jail on 30 April pending trial on a charge of 'armed hooliganism', on the condition he does not leave the city. Galeev was arrested on 27 May 1998 after Interior Ministry officers raided Titan, following demands from Ufa's mayor Fidus Yamaletdinov that its owner dissolve his lease. Galeev was arrested after he fired a shot from a gas gun following the removal of the station's transmitter and phone lines. (GDF)

SAUDI ARABIA

Seventy-year-old journalist **Ishaq al-Sheikh Yaqub** was arrested on 11 April as he returned from Bahrain across the King Fahd Causeway, taken to

prison and reportedly beaten during questioning. He has not been informed of any charge against him or when he will be brought to trial. He has no access to a lawyer. (AI, Movement for Islamic Reform in Arabia)

On 14 April the London-based Al-Jeel ('the Current Generation') TV station was cut off by ANN TV, following pressure from the government. Al-Jeel and two US companies, The Link and NUJ, had rented time on ANN's subcarrier SMS, but were suddenly disconnected. After five days of silence, ANN told SMS that the service had been discontinued because of 'biased political material', adding that the Saudi embassy had threatened to restrict ANN's access to the Kingdom and the rest of the Persian Gulf. Al-Jeel had recently changed its broadcasting from music only, to include a discussion on the potential successor to the Grand Mufti. (Movement for Islamic Reform in Arabia)

SERBIA-MONTENEGRO

On 10 April the Montenegrin government rejected a Yugoslav Second Army demand to ban the rebroadcasting of foreign radio programmes in Serbian-Croatian, on the basis that they 'in no way adversely affected national defence'. (RFE/RL)

On 13 April the formerly independent Radio B92 went back on the air, three weeks after it was banned by authorities. Under new, pro-Milosevic management it now broadcasts news from official news sources and Serbian music. (RFE/RL)

On 14 June two correspondents for the German magazine *Stern*, **Volker Krämer** and **Gabriel Grüner**, were killed by Serbs while driving through Dulje, a village midway between Pristina and Prizren, the base for about 8,000 German NATO troops. Krämer died instantly and Grüner later in a Macedonian hospital. A third member of the party, their translator **Senol Alit**, was also shot. Reports said the journalists were lured out of their car with a promise that they would be taken to the site of a mass grave. *(IFJ, International Herald Tribune, Guardian)*

On 22 April the Albanian-language daily *Koha Ditore* resumed publication from Macedonia. On the same day, the paper and its editor, **Baton Haixhu**, were convicted of publishing information that 'incited hatred between nationalities' according to the controversial Law on Public Information (*Index* 3/1999). The paper was fined 420,000 dinars (US$ 26,800) and Haixhu 110,000 dinars (US$ 7,200). (Association of Independent Electronic Media)

On 23 April the Sokobanja District Court found **Nebojsa Ristic**, editor of TV Soko, guilty of 'disseminating false information' under Article 218 of the Penal Code after he publicly displyed a poster, with a Radio B92 stamp, saying 'Free Press Made in Serbia!' He was sentenced to one year in prison.

His lawyers filed an appeal but Ristic is still in detention pending proceedings. (Association of Independent Electronic Media)

On 23 April the IFJ condemned NATO's attack on Serbian State television, warning that the action could lead to reprisals against independent journalists and media staff. (IFJ)

Serbian threats and the use of military courts forced two Montenegrin journalists into hiding in early May. **Nebojsa Redzic**, editor-in-chief of the independent radio station Radio Free Montenegro, stands accused of broadcasting news that 'weakened the army's defence power' by carrying reports of the NATO bombing. **Miodrag Perovic**, founder of the weekly magazine *Monitor* and the radio station Antenna M, has been charged with 'violating the integrity of Yugoslavia' and 'interfering with the fight against the enemy'. Their whereabouts remain unknown. On 11 May, the military court also attempted to issue a summons to *Monitor* journalist **Beba Marusic**. A statement broadcast on Montenegrin TV pleaded 'only the Montenegrin civilian authorities and courts are competent to say whether journalists have violated the laws of the country'. The use of military courts to try civilian journalists breaks the Geneva Conventions. (A19)

On 7 May **Vyacheslav Grunsky**, a correspondent with Russia's independent NTV network, was expelled from

Yugoslavia with no explanation from Serbian officials. NTV management claim the move came as retaliation for NTV's reports on human rights violations by Serb forces in Kosovo. (CPJ)

On 9 May **Juha Metso**, a photographer with the Finnish daily *Helsingin Sanomat*, was arrested and severely beaten by Serbian police near the Morina border post on the Albanian border. He was stopped on the Albanian side at the same spot where freelance photographer **Samuel Bolandorff** was assaulted by Serbian police on 4 April. Metso was taking photographs of refugees when he was struck with a truncheon and taken to a room at the border post for interrogation. The officers forced Metso to undress, threatened to kill him and confiscated his films. (RSF)

On 10 May the International Federation of Journalists (IFJ) launched a programme of assistance for Serbian journalists, following the death of the three reporters in the NATO bombing of the Chinese embassy in Belgrade. **Xu Xinghu** and **Zhu Ying** of *Guangming Daily* and **Shao Yuhuan** of Xinhua News Agency were 'in the embassy because they considered it to be the safest place for them in Belgrade' said Aidan White, general secretary of the IFJ. The IFJ estimates that at least 20 journalists have died either as victims of assassination or in the NATO bombing campaign. (IFJ, Hong Kong Journalists Association)

Pit Schnitzler, a correspondent with German television channel SAT-1, was released on 11 May after international appeals. Schnitzler was detained on 16 April between Belgrade and the Serbian-Croatian border, eight days after his car and equipment were taken at gunpoint by police officers in the garage of the Belgrade Intercontinental hotel, despite his official receipt for the equipment. He was originally charged with espionage and beaten badly in his first week in captivity. One other journalist is missing: **Antun Masle**, of the Croatian weekly *Globus,* disappeared on 21 April. (IFJ, CPJ)

On 18 April **Ojukutu-Macauley**, Freetown correspondent for the BBC, interviewed rebel leader Foday Sankoh – who was conditionally released the same day to attend peace talks in Togo – for that evening's broadcast of the programme *Focus on Africa*. On 20 April the state-owned Sierra Leone Broadcasting Service aired several programmes which accused Ojukutu-Macauley of fabricating statements by Sankoh. (CPJ)

On 30 April *Expo Times* news editor **Conrad Roy** died at the Lakka Tuberculosis Hospital. Roy contracted TB while in prison. He was detained by the West African Peacekeeping Force (ECOMOG) in February 1998, but not charged until December 1998. He was accused of treason, aiding and abetting the enemy and conspiring to overthrow a legally constituted government. (CPJ)

On 5 May three journalists from the *New Storm* weekly newspaper were arrested after publication of an article suggesting that ECOMOG was not committed to peace in the region. **Ahmed Kanneh, Thomas Gbow** and **Mohammad Massaquoi**, publisher, editor and news editor respectively, were released on a combined bail of 5 million leones (US$2,400) on 13 May. (CPJ)

On 8 May Information Minister Julius Spencer announced that all newspapers must register with the ministry by 14 May and pay any outstanding taxes to continue publishing. The government recently increased the special tax on the media by approximately 280 per cent. (CPJ).

On 18 May two ECOMOG officers detained **Johnathan Leigh**, managing editor of the *Observer* newspaper, on the orders of Major Tanko, following an article alleging that troops under Tanko's command had conducted searches for weapons. (CPJ)

On 13 May internet provider SingNet apologised to its subscribers after scanning their PCs without their knowledge. The company asked the Home Affairs ministry to help check the computers of its 200,000 subscribers in the wake of the damage caused by the CIH virus. An anti-hacking programme used by a customer picked up the intrusion, which was reported to the police. The police then traced the scan back to the government. SingNet claimed no confidential files were interrogated, athough they did find over 900 virus-infected computers. (*Daily Telegraph*)

Poet **Mzwake Mbuli** was sentenced to 13 years for armed robbery and five years for possession of a hand grenade (*Index* 6/1998, 3/1999). Mbuli claims he was framed by the South African police to prevent him from speaking out against corruption. (WiPC)

Around 300 members of a sect stormed the premises of the Munhwa Broadcasting Corporation on 13 May, disrupting a television programme on alleged corruption by a religious leader. Followers of the People's Central Holy Church, which claims about 65,000 members, burst into the control room and cut the power, stopping the transmission of the programme five minutes after it had gone on air. The Korean Federation of Churches has accused the government of failing to look into allegations of wrongdoing by religious groups and urged prosecution authoritites to investigate the church. (Associated Press, Reuters)

SRI LANKA

On 5 May **Srilal Priyantha**, a reporter for the Sinhala-language *Lakbima* newspaper, was arrested by police on charges of murdering five people during a Marxist insurrection in the late 1980s. According to the police, Priyantha's involvement came to light after he was abducted, beaten and left for dead by suspected members of the military in March (*Index* 3/1999). When his photos appeared in public, residents of his hometown near Colombo were reportedly shocked, having believed that Priyantha had died 10 years before. Priyantha has denied the allegations, arguing that they are an attempt by the security forces to get back for his articles about corruption and abuse of power in the military. (Reuters, Associated Press, Asian Human Rights Commission)

Recent Publications: *Background Paper On Sri Lanka – For the European Union High Level Working Group On Asylum And Migration* (United Nations High Commissioner For Refugees, March 1999, pp 25); *Sri Lanka: Torture in custody*(AI, June 1999)

SUDAN

On 14 April **Mohammed Abdel Alseed**, a correspondent with the London-based daily *Asharq Al-Aswat*, was detained at his home in Khartoum for allegedly breaching security. Alseed was released without charge or trial on 26 May with wounds on his arms and legs as a result of severe torture. This was

the third time that the journalist had been detained. (RSF, AI)

On or around the same date, **Abdel Al-Gadir Hafiz**, a correspondent for the Saudi newspaper *Al-Gezira*, was detained and questioned about his alleged spying activities. He was releaed without charge on 23 April. (AI)

Mutasim Mahmoud, the chief editor of Khartoum daily *Al ray Alaam*, was arrested on 17 April by security forces and detained at an unknown locality. (Reuters, OMCT)

On 18 April **Maha Hassan Ali**, a senior reporter at the official Sudan News Agency (Suna), was arrested at her home in Al Kalakla. Ali was released on 23 April without charge. She had been questioned over allegations that she was a spy for a foreign country. (Reuters, Agence France Presse, OMCT)

In the week of 20 May, the military authorities demolished two Christian church buildings and two schools at Hayy Barakah, a Khartoum suburb, in what displaced Christians from the south claim is religious victimisation. The two schools, owned by Episcopal Church of Sudan and the Presbyterian Church, had a combined roll of 1,400 students. (BBC)

Recent Publications: Zwier, Lawrence J., 1998, *North Against South (World in Conflict)* Lemer Publications; *Food and power in Sudan – A critique of humanitarianism* (African Rights, May 1997 372pp)

SYRIA

It was reported on 20 April that the missing journalist **'Adel Ismaíl** was allegedly arrested in 1996 upon arrival from Algeria. It is not known whether he has been tried but he is believed to be jailed in Seydnaya and it is feared that he has been tortured. At least 10 journalists, sentenced to between eight and 15 years and often to hard labour as well, are believed to be imprisoned for non-violent 'offences'. In most critical condition is **Nizar Nayyouf**, editor-in-chief of *Sawt al-Democratiyya* ('Democratic Voice'), who is reported to have been severely tortured, denied medical treatment and is in danger of dying. Nayyouf is also suffering from leukaemia, but has been denied treatment until he acknowledges that 'he made false declarations concerning the situation of human rights in Syria'. (RSF, WAN)

Poet **Faraj Ahmad Birqdar**, one of the longest-detained writers in the world, was awarded the 1999 PEN/Barbara Goldsmith Freedom-to-Write Award on 11 May. Birqdar was sentenced in 1993 to 15 years, having already been held without charge for more than six. He was arrested in 1987 on suspicion of belonging to the Party for Communist Action. (PEN)

TANZANIA

Twenty-eight members of the International Freedom of Expression Exchange (IFEX) on

April 23 signed a joint action calling on the Zanzibar government to remove a ban on **Mwinyi Saddala** (*Index* 2/1999) who was prevented from reporting from the island. Saddala filed for the private news agency. Press Service of Tanzania. (Media Institute of South Africa)

The ruling Chama Cha Mapinduzi (CCM) on 12 May threatened to take the private daily *Heko* to court over a report which apparently outlined part of the party's election strategy for the year 2000. The party claimed that the story carried on 3 May was aimed at 'creating hatred and misunderstanding in society'. (Media Institute of South Africa)

TOGO

On 4 April police officers who had been criticised in the newspaper *Tingo-Tingo* went to the newspaper's offices and beat up a number of journalists. (UJIT, West Africa Journalists Association)

On 12 April, copies of the newspaper *Le Combat du Peuple* were seized at newspaper stands. (UJIT, West Africa Journalists Association)

On 19 April **Romain Koudjodji**, editor-in-chief of the newspaper *Le Reporter*, was arrested at his home and transferred to Lomé civilian prison a day later. Koudjodji is charged with publishing an article which claimed that the police had tortured a member of the opposition Comité d'Action

pour le Renouveau. (UJIT, West Africa Journalists Association)

The editors-in-chief of the publications *Le Regard* and *Nouvel Echo* went into hiding in mid-April following threats of violence after the publication of articles critical of the government on 19 and 23 April. (UJIT, West Africa Journalists Association)

Two journalists with the paper *Le Nouveau Combat*, **Elias Hounkanly** and **Agbéko Amewouho**, who spent eight and five months in prison respectively, were sent for trial on 28 April. They received three-month suspended sentences, a one million CFA franc fine (approx. US$1,700) and a symbolic one franc fine to the presidential couple. They were released at the end of the trial. The reporters were arrested in August and November 1998 (*Index* 6/1998) for an article concerning jewellery allegedly left in trust with First Lady Gnassingbé Eyadéma by Madame Mobutu Sese Seko, widow of the former Zairean dictator, in 1997. (AI, UJIT)

TUNISIA

On 28 April **Taufik Ben Brick**, a correspondent for the French daily *La Croix* and press agency SYFIA, was stopped and had his passport confiscated as he was about to travel to a conference in Switzerland. On 20 May Taufik was attacked in the street by plainclothes police officers who allegedly beat him. Four days later he was again arrested and detained for several

hours. Ben Brick has increasingly been harassed because of his criticism of the suppression of human rights and press freedom (*Index* 5/1998, 2/1999). (HRW, RSF)

TURKEY

Two teenagers, **Yilmaz** and **Mehmet Elustu**, were killed by police and members of the special forces in the predominantly Kurdish southeast, it was reported on 19 April. They were handing out material for the pro-Kurdish HADEP during the election campaign, when they were shot from behind. Their bodies were then blown up with hand grenades. The local military commander reportedly apologised for this 'mistake'. (*Evrensel*, German Election Observation Team report)

On 30 April the country's highest-ranking judge, **Ahmet Necdet Sezer**, urged parliament to repeal a series of constitutional provisions, including the ban on teaching the Kurdish language which, he said, violated international agreements. He was speaking to an audience of lawyers and ministers at the constitutional court's 37th anniversary celebrations. Sezer called for changes in laws which limit the freedom of political parties, labour unions and the press. He also urged relaxation of the notorious 'Anti-Terror' laws which punish statements deemed to encourage violence. (*New York Times*)

On 6 May writer and publisher

Muzaffer Ilhan Erdost was sentenced to a year in prison on charges relating to his book *Three Sivas*. Erdost was first imprisoned in the 1970s as publisher of the Sol Publishing House. His present conviction is for writing about three incidents in Sivas town, where citizens were massacred. Erdost can be e-mailed: ilhankit@prizma.net.tr. (PEN)

At the 25th and final hearing in the trial of **Metin Goktepe**'s killers on 6 May, the court sentenced six police officers to seven and a half years in jail for 'involuntary homicide'. Goktepe, a journalist with the daily *Evrensel*, was beaten to death in a sports stadium on 8 January 1996 (*Index* 2/1996, 1/1997, 6/1997, 1/1998, 2/1998, 3/1998, 5/1998, 1/1999, 2/1999). (RSF)

On 18 May journalist **Oral Calislar** was sentenced to 13 months in prison under the Anti-Terror Laws for a 1993 book, *The Kurdish Problem with Ocalan and Burkey*. The book contained interviews with **Kemal Burkey**, head of the moderate Kurdistan Socialist Party, and **Abdullah Oçalan**, leader of the outlawed Kurdistan Workers' Party. Calislar, a columnist for the broadsheet *Cumhuriyet*, has been on trial for six years. The new prime minister, Bulent Ecevit, said he was deeply saddened by the verdict and hoped the decision would be repealed by the supreme court. (Reuters, CPJ, International Press Institute)

President Suleyman Demirel endorsed a government decision on 15 May to revoke the citizenship of Virtue Party deputy **Merve Kavaci** for becoming an American citizen without informing the authorities. Kavaci earlier caused a storm in parliament by taking her swearing-in oath in an Islamic headscarf. (*Turkish Daily News*)

Dissident academic and writer **Yalcin Kucuk** was sentenced on 14 May to 16 months in prison for a speech he had made on the exiled Kurdish television station Med-TV (*Index*, 1/1999). Journalist and writer **Haluk Gerger** was acquitted in the same case. (*Turkish Daily News*)

A telegram of solidarity to the Ankara District Congress of the HADEP party may earn **Leyla Zana** (*Index*,1/1997, 6/1998) and her fellow Kurdish MPs further legal proceedings before the Ankara State Security Court. Since March 1994, all have been serving 15-year jail terms for 'crimes of thought'. On 24 May, in the course of a hearing held in the absence of the accused, the public prosecutor demanded five years' imprisonment for Leyla Zana, Hatip Dicle, Orhan Dogan and Selim Sadak, all accused of separatist propaganda in a short telegrammed message they sent to the Congress in May 1998. The prosecutor also called for sentences of three to five years for the five musicians of the **Group Mezopotamya**, accused of singing in Kurdish at a cultural evening event organised at the end of the Congress. Their trial has been set for the end of June. (*Cildekt*)

On 4 June **Akin Birdal** (*Index* 4/1998, 5/1998, 1/1999), president of the Human Rights Association, was sent to prison to serve the sentence passed on him in June 1998 for a speech on World Peace Day calling for an end to the war in Turkey. Human Rights Watch condemned the imprisonment as a violation of his right to free speech. The sentence includes a ban on his presidency of the HRA and as an official of any association. Last year Akin Birdal survived an assassination attack. (HRW, *Turkish Daily News*)

UGANDA

Three journalists with the independent daily *Monitor* were detained on 13 May by the criminal investigation department and charged with sedition. **Wafula Oguttu**, editor-in-chief, **Charles Onyango-Obbo**, editor and news editor **David Ouma Balikow** were charged with publishing a photograph depicting soldiers holding a nude woman while one soldier held a pair of scissors near her genital area. The caption said the shot was taken near an army barracks in the northern city of Gulu. (*Monitor*)

UKRAINE

On 16 May **Igor Bondar**, director of the AMT television station, was shot and killed as he was driving in a car in Odessa with **Boris Vikhrov**, the city court's presiding judge who was also killed. (RSF)

• •

YILMAZ ODABASI
Charge: Separatist Propaganda

'The laws of 12 September [1980, the date of the last military coup] institutionalised fascism in a subtle manner. Inflation dangled like a Sword of Damocles over the lives of the labourers; human dignity was for sale; and it was believed that the screams of Kurdish people, under the coercion of state terror, could be trained into silence through blood, rifle butts, migration and poverty.'

Charge: Separatist Propaganda
'From the time of Mustafa Suphi [founder of the Turkish Communist Party in the 1920s] to now, the 70-year heritage of the Left could not be changed in an appropriate way. New and functional practices for transforming the shattered consciousness of the new human concept that emerged from new social and political processes have not been initiated.'

Charge: Violating 'The Law to Protect Ataturk'
'Did Kemalism not murder Mustafa Suphi and his comrades? Did Kemalism not imprison [the poet] Nazim Hikmet for years on the grounds he was a communist? Were not tens of thousands of people murdered in horrifying circumstances, including those in the south-eastern province of Dersim and during the Sheikh Said rebellion, by order of Mustafa Kemal and under the special care of officials like Fethi Okyar. Were hundreds of villages not burnt?'

Charge: Separatist Propaganda
'In 1996 in Diyarbakir, there is no such thing as a "labour class"! People are either peasants or unemployed or civil servants. When blood is shed for the Kurdish identity, if you promise people a future by labelling political concepts – all versions of Kemalism – as "socialism" or "labour", they laugh at you, believe me. Because the dynamics of the struggle are nourished in a different direction'

Charge: Separatist Propaganda
'As long as the prohibition of [freedom of] thought continues, and as long as the Kurdish people are not free, it is of no importance whether or not my book achieves success or sells a lot of copies. It means that I am under oppression.'

• •

Two women on opposite poles

'I am a defender of the women's movement. I believe that women are oppressed and deprived of their rights. I support their emergence in civic life.

When Çiller became prime minister, women were very happy. "Now that a prime minister has emerged from among us, male-dominated society will somehow change," they thought. I viewed this with scepticism. I thought that somebody who chanted "'Flag, *Ezan*, Quran'" and acted in chauvinist manner could not gain victories [valuable] for the female gender.

In an article about Tansu Çiller, I wrote : "She does not belong to any gender. She is a ghost; do ghosts have sexuality?"

I really do not believe that she belongs to any sex. I think women are more affectionate, have more motherly feelings and that breast-feeding and hosting the child in the womb create very private emotions. Çiller is a mother but, having hosted a child, she should have deeper responses when it comes to the screaming of women and the agony of the young, regardless of whether they are Turkish boys or [Kurdish] guerrillas.

Peace in the Kurdish question is in our hands. Peace is so close, but when the question is referred to the military, we face such pain. The pain has been manifold and the hearts of mothers were tormented. The screams rise to the level of a high mountain, but the attitude of "blood for blood" still applies.

Somebody who applies such an attitude has committed a great sin. She becomes a ghost and has nothing to do with gender.

Leyla Zana [an imprisoned MP of the moderate Kurdish parliamentary party HADEP] is a person I like and respect a lot. She is really a courageous woman. The speech she gave in parliament has touched me enormously. She said: 'I take this oath for the fraternity of Turkish and Kurdish peoples.' People should have embraced the words. We should all have embraced!' ❏

Yilmaz Odabasi, a prize-winning poet, writer and journalist, was sent to Bursa Prison on 12 March 1999 to serve an 18-month term for 'insulting Mustafa Kemal Ataturk, founder of the Turkish Republic' in his volume of poetry Dream and Life, *published in 1996. He was found innocent of the charge 'separatist propaganda'. Odabasi's previous volumes of poetry include* Poems Without Land, Times of Plunder *and* Melody from the Same Sky. *He won the Cahit Sitki Taranci prize in 1989.*
Translation by Umit Ozturk.

UNITED KINGDOM

The BBC stepped up staff security on 29 April after telephone threats from an alleged Serbian terror group, which claimed responsibility for the assassination of the popular presenter **Jill Dando**. Executives **Tony Hall** and **Alan Yentob** and *Today* presenter **John Humphrys** were all targets, said a caller who added that the BBC had been chosen because it was the 'voice of government'. (*Guardian*)

On 12 May a website based in the US published a list of 116 intelligence operatives from the UK's intelligence service MI6. The publication spurred the Foreign Office into calling for the closure of the site, which was later withdrawn by the ISP, though not before it had been mirrored elsewhere on the web. Former MI6 agent **Richard Tomlinson**, who had been sentenced to six months' imprisonment for breaching the Official Secrets Act, was widely reported as responsible for the leak. (*International Herald Tribune, Guardian, Daily Telegraph*)

A Cabinet Office letter, leaked by Friends of the Earth (FOE) on 20 May, intensified public debate over genetically modified (GM) food by revealing that the government had tried to arrange for an 'independent' scientist to rebut consumer fears on the BBC's influential *Today* programme. FOE claimed that the letter demonstrated the government's desire to 'spin GM foods down our throats whether

we like it or not'. (*Guardian, Daily Telegraph*)

On 24 May the government finally unveiled draft legislation on a Freedom of Information bill, a Labour manifesto pledge for 20 years. The bill was far weaker than voters had been led to believe. Information on the formulation of policy is exempted under the legislation and civil servants are likely to insist that other categories fall under the same interdict. Industry benefits with the exemption from the draft of any information likely to harm 'commercial interests'. Exemption is also extended to any topic of enquiry that 'would prejudice the effective conduct of public affairs'. (*Daily Telegraph, Financial Times*)

USA

On 12 April an unidentified group filled newspaper racks with an unofficial, four-page supplement to the *San Francisco Chronicle*. The doctored edition sported a bogus front page, entitled the *San Francisco Chomical*, and demanded freedom for **Mumia Abu-Jamal**, the black activist sentenced to death for the 1981 killing of police officer Daniel Faulkner (*Index* 2/1995, 6/1995, 2/1996, 6/1996, 1/1997, 2/1999). (*San Francisco Bay Guardian*)

On 29 April a US state appeals court ruled that the state cannot fire **Edward Kuhnel**, a prison guard who flew a Nazi flag from his home. Kuhnel was suspended in 1996 from the Eastern

Correctional Facility where the population is 50 per cent black and 30 per cent Hispanic. He remains on the payroll and been paid US$103,180 since his suspension. (Freedom Forum)

On 3 May *The Jenny Jones Show* was ordered to pay £15.7 million to the family of **Scott Amedure** who was killed by Jonathan Schmidt after the pair appeared on the chat show. In the 1995 broadcast, Amedure confessed to his homosexual feelings for his neighbour Schmidt, who later shot him dead. (*Daily Telegraph*)

On 4 May a federal appeals court ruled that Circuit Judge Thomas C Platt had violated the civil rights of **Lester K. Coleman** who was imprisoned and fined for five counts of perjury for the 1991 affidavit he had given in the Lockerbie disaster civil case. Coleman had claimed he was a former agent with the Defense Intelligence Agency and that the Lockerbie tragedy was caused by a US drug sting operation that went wrong. Coleman reiterated these allegations in the book, *Trail of the Octopus*. At the time of publication, he and his family were living in Sweden, having successfully applied for political asylum. When Coleman voluntarily returned to the US in 1996 he was held without bail for five months, during which he developed a cancerous tumour. Denied proper medical attention, his condition deteriorated. Dr Jim Swire, spokesman for the British relatives of the Lockerbie victims, wrote: 'The gross maltreatment of Coleman by the authorities appears to fit a pattern of victimisation of people who challenge the official version that Libya was solely to blame for Lockerbie.' Coleman has filed a US$6.5 million damage suit against the US prison service for ill-treatment during his time in jail. (Coleman Family Fund)

On 4 June **Kathy Scruggs** and **Ron Martz**, reporters with the *Atlanta Journal-Constitution*, were sentenced by Judge John Mather to an indeterminate period in prison for refusing to reveal their sources for stories about former Olympic Games bombing suspect, Richard Jewell. Jewell, initially lauded for spotting a bomb at the Centennial Olympic Park in July 1996, sued the paper in January 1997 after the reporters' allegations about his 'strange work history' and the disclosure that he was the subject of a criminal investigation in the case. Mather first ordered Scruggs and Martz to reveal their sources – presumed to be law enforcement officials – in April 1998. (*Atlanta Journal-Constitution*)

VANUATU

On 29 April it was reported that a former business associate of Deputy Prime Minister Willy Jimmy assaulted the *Vanuatu Trading Post* publisher **Marc Neal-Jones** at a popular nightspot. Jimmy was talking to Neal-Jones at the time, the paper said, but was not involved in the attack. The *Trading Post* later received a threatening call warning it not to write about

Jimmy's involvement in the assault. (*Daily Telegraph*)

VIETNAM

The National Assembly has passed a press law giving the ministry of culture and information sole responsibility for all media outlets, including the Internet. One provision requires compensation to be paid to anyone hurt by a report, even if it is proven accurate. (WAN)

On 13 April the ministry for foreign affairs confirmed that geologist and writer **Nguyen Thanh Giang**, arrested in Hanoi on 4 March (*Index* 3/1999), was officially charged with violating Article 205A of the Penal Code, for 'abusing freedom of speech, of the press or of religion ... to encroach upon the interests of the State'. No trial date has been set.

YEMEN

On 10 May four masked and armed men beat up **Saif al-Haderi**, editor-in-chief of the weekly *Al-Shummua*, before fleeing the scene. He was later hospitalised for his injuries. Haderi is an outspoken critic of government officials. (CPJ)

ZAMBIA

On 21 May the Lusaka High Court awarded Ludwig Sondashu, secretary general of Zambia's National Party (NP), K30 million (US$12,000) in damages following an action against the now-defunct *Sun* newspaper. The case follows an article printed in the *Sun*

entitled 'Sondashi deserves to ne expelled'. (MISA)

ZIMBABWE

President Robert Mugabe said in an interview with the *Sunday Mail* on 25 April that he intends to strengthen state powers against the media. Mugabe claimed that journalists enjoy a status higher than 'gods or angels' but that they will be prevented from using their pen 'as a bloody sword'. (MISA)

Journalists **Mark Chavunduka** and **Ray Choto** (*Index* 3/1999), whose medical reports confirmed that they had been tortured while in military detention, began civil and criminal actions against the police and military in late May. Chavunduka and Choto, editor and senior reporter of the *Standard* newspaper respectively, were arrested following the publication of a 10 January article alleging an aborted coup by the military. They are currently on bail and have had their passports and security bonds returned. The next trial date is set for 2 August. (Media Institute of South Africa)

Compiled by: Jake Barnes, John Kamau, Daniel Rogers (Africa); Rupert Clayton, Andrew Kendle, Alex Lockwood, Jon Parr (Asia); Alex Lockwood, Simon Martin (eastern Europe and CIS); Dolores Cortés, Daniel Rogers (south and central America); Arif Azad, Gill Newsham, Neil Sammonds (Middle East); Billie Felix Jeyes (north America and Pacific); Tony Callaghan (UK and western Europe).

IVO ZANIC

New myths for old

The Kosovo legend is only one of the many myths that bedevil the modern history of the Balkans

The collapse of Yugoslavia naturally and inevitably entailed and demanded the examination and reinterpretation of the history of all the nations or countries of which it had been composed or which emerged from it. It is impossible to exaggerate the importance such a process has for the democratic development of the whole region. The replacement of old myths with new ones is spontaneously experienced as demythologisation, or is represented as such by the new political elites. This is a trap it is easier to fall into than avoid. The central question is therefore: how to develop resistance to new myths, how to learn to recognise what is always the same structure which, like so many other phenomena, is characterised by the fact that it is incomparably easier to recognise (and condemn) in others than in oneself.

The Kosovo legend has seen periods of blossoming and periods of decline; the emphasis in different circumstances has shifted from one to another of the elements it comprises. Its greatest transformation has been its connection to the Old Testament theme of a chosen people. Regardless of all its factual uncertainties and proven inaccuracies, the Battle of Kosovo in 1389 has become, in the common consciousness, the central event of Serbian national history.

Along with all the changes it has undergone and is still undergoing, it has permeated Serbian culture, political thought and public life to a degree and with a continuous intensity – and enduringly disastrous consequences – unparalleled in recent European history.

Nevertheless, one intriguing fact is striking in this context: while the public have been flooded with plays, poems and pamphlets, ideological articles and political speeches, (para) theological and (para) liturgical

Serb anti-NATO demonstration – Credit: Rex/Ray Tang

interpretations and narratives, as endless variations on the themes of national unity and disunity, belief and unbelief, betrayal, sacrifice and heroism, historical messianism and national mystification, in early Serbian art there was no monumental work illustrating the Kosovo battle.

In the second half of the last century, at a time of strong national exaltation, the Kosovo myth had provided the stimulus for such an outburst of hatred first against the Turks, and then against the so-called 'Turks' – that is Muslim Albanians and Bosnians – that the most influential literary critic of the time, Jovan Skerlic, even spoke of a prevailing 'cannibalistic mood'. In the preparations, military as much as psychological, for the first Balkan war, the Kosovo myth was used to construct above all an ethics of duty and sacrifice (with the emphasis on the former). Later, in the course of World War I, with the loss of territory, including the recently acquired Kosovo, and the retreat of the army and people through Albania, the stress shifted more forcefully to sacrifice and victimhood. When the army was waiting on the Salonica Front preparing to break through the lines, these two principles achieved a rough equilibrium.

In more recent times, the myth experienced its most intensive realisation and culmination as a carefully orchestrated project involving virtually the whole political, artistic and church elite of Serbia in 1989. This was the 600th anniversary of the battle; the myth then acquired the sense of moral triumph of the victim who refuses to submit. And those endeavouring to impose submission on the Serbs had to be resisted with a moral superiority which, in the nature of things, *a priori* excluded the possibility of itself committing any mistake, injustice or even crime. The role of subjugator was assigned to all those with whom the Serbs had lived, up to then, in a shared state.

As a concrete narrative, with a concrete locality, characters, situations and messages, irrespective of how far they are historically reliable, the Kosovo story is only a Serbian myth. And this is how it will remain until the Serbs themselves see through it; until they confront those of its

aspects which have for decades prevented them from placing their
assumptions about themselves, their neighbours and their place in the
world in remotely realistic categories. It is those aspects of the myth that
have fatally blocked the modernisation of their society. In this process,
no one can replace them or help them in a fundamental way.

But the Kosovo myth, reduced to its basic structure, is a universal
fact. All the myths of the world are in a certain way also Kosovo myths.
In all of them, human communities interpret themselves, their historical
path and the reasons for the end of their former golden age of harmony
and greatness. The French thinker Maurice Drouon says that if peoples
had not had legends and myths they would have frozen in the winter of
history. In this sense, myth is a form of remembering that inspires and
strengthens a community in difficult times. In the same way, individuals
encourage themselves at times of crisis with recollections of former good
times, whether real or imagined.

Myth always functions in the same way: it selects from the past those
events it is important to transform in the interests of creating a simple
and coherent story. In this essence and function, the model does not
change. There are differences, however, in the intensity with which it is
present in a society and in the degree to which it influences that society's
political decisions and value judgments. There are differences, too, in the
extent to which it reaches the broad public, above all the so-called silent
majority. And in the degree to which the boundary between a rational
and mythical interpretation of reality is blurred, which activities it affects
and which segments of society or institutions support it and affect its
development in a direction that suits their interests.

In the final analysis, it can have widely different effects: some work of
art inspired by its themes that enriches the culture of that nation for
ever; a greater or lesser number of contributions to The Greatest Shits;
but also heaps of corpses and endless smouldering ruins. These effects are
its essential – indeed its only – historical and moral measure.

In the case of the Kosovo myth, its value in principle is contained in
the balanced and precise – and for the later development of Serbia,
prophetic – conclusion of the literary historian, Miodrag Popovic, in
1976:

> 'The Vidovdan cult [the battle of Kosovo was on St Vitus' Day, 28
> June – Translator], which mixes historical fact with mythic reality,
> a real battle for freedom with traces of pagan tendencies (revenge,

slaughter, ritual sacrifice, the resurrection of an heroic forebear), potentially contains all the characteristics of a milieu with untamed mythic impulses. As a certain phase in the development of national thought, it was historically indispensable. But, as an enduring state of mind, the Vidovdan cult may also be fateful for those who are not in a position to extract themselves from its pseudomythic and pseudohistorical web. And in that web, contemporary thought a the human spirit may experience a new Kosovo, intellectual and ethical defeat.'

Historical reality is far more complex and 'illogical' than myth-makers could ever imagine. It is always able to compose some 'dramatic combination' and fling it in the face of the falsifiers and propagandists. History has mocked the Serbian myth of Kosovo like this in a truly masterful way.

Namely, a large part of Serbian state and political thinking has been, for more than a century, focused on 'avenging Kosovo'. But although a series of historical situations, from political turning points to armed conflicts, have been interpreted in that light, in Kosovo itself, since the mythic year of 1389, the Serbian army had no conflict with the Ottoman army which could be interpreted in mythic categories as a direct 'vengeance for Kosovo', as payment for that defeat. The battle in the first Balkan war which was seen as the longed-for vengeance for Kosovo, took place not in Kosovo but near Kumanovo, in Macedonia, where the Serbian army defeated the Turkish army in 1912. The slogan of the day was 'Kumanovo for Kosovo'.

Nevertheless, it was precisely in Kosovo, near Lipljane, a little south of the mythic Gazimestan [site of the battle of Kosovo, 1389 – Translator], that the Turks experienced a major defeat. But it was not at the hands of the Serbs, nor even of Christians, but of someone so unexpected that, from today's perspective, one can really talk of a textbook example of historical irony (or a lesson, if it were the case that anyone, ever, learnt anything from history). This battle took place relatively recently, in the summer of 1831, when the Turkish Sultan sent a powerful army to quell an uprising in Bosnia. The leader of the uprising, the 'Bosnian Dragon', Husein-beg Gradascevic from Gradacac, set out to meet it with an army of Bosnian Muslims, and inflicted a fundamental defeat on the Turks, of a kind that Dobrica Cosic and Vuk Draskovic could only dream about.

In other words, Prince Lazar [the Serbian leader killed at Kosovo – Translator] and Milos Obilic [the Serbian hero who slew Murat, the Turkish Sultan – Tr] were avenged by precisely those whom in this century Great Serbdom under the slogan of 'Vengeance for Kosovo', has systematically exterminated as 'Turks', bloodily and collectively accused of the 'defeat of the Serbian empire' [the title of one of the traditional songs in the Kosovo cycle – Tr] at Kosovo in 1389.

What is more, Bosnian Muslim national ideology at the end of the nineteenth century interpreted the battle in exactly this way. Its main protagonist, the poet Safvet-beg Basagic, wrote in the Romantic spirit of the time a little history, *The Bosnians in Kosovo*. In this, he expressly emphasised the identity of the two historical situations: just as the Sultan in 1389 attacked the Serbs in their homeland, so they were now attacking the Bosnians in theirs.

As he led the Bosnian army towards Kosovo, the battleground reminded Gradiscevic of 'the fate of the Serbs'. And it was precisely in that fact that the Bosnians found new motivation and entered the battle with the cry that 'the cursed bloodletting was being avenged by the sons on the sons of the fathers'. That is to say, they, the Muslim Bosnians, were not only defending their land in a concrete historical situation, but they were doing it in the name of Slav solidarity and a shared Slav origin. They were also taking on themselves the redeeming task of paying back, in symbolic historic time, the defeat the Sultan's army had inflicted on their Slav brethren, the Orthodox Serbs.

From the point of view of the prevailing ideology of Slav mutuality at that time, faith was quite immaterial: the Bosnians were above all a Slav people, and as such had full moral, historical and political legitimacy to punish the same non-Slav conqueror who had once brought such misfortune to another, brotherly, Slav people.

Today, we are witnessing the disintegration of the Kosovo myth and with it the ideological construction of Greater Serbia, whose phantasms have led the Serbs and Serbia to war with almost all their neighbours and, in the end, brought the greatest long-term catastrophe upon themselves. At this time, we should bear in mind that the collapse of the Greater Serbian idea, however necessary it is, will actually solve little if the moral of its historical blind alley is not drawn, not only by the Serbs, but also by their neighbours.

First, its physical defeat does not imply that the mentality that fostered it has also automatically and inevitably been defeated. Otherwise, we could see a repetition of the situation of a decade ago, when many well-intentioned Croats believed that freedom was nothing other than the mechanical negation of Yugoslavia and communism; that freedom would be established naturally the moment those two factors were removed, one way or another, physically or formally; and that with their removal all questions would be for ever solved.

Second, regardless of the relief and satisfaction one feels, after all that has happened, that Milosevic's criminal machine has begun to collapse under NATO bombs, there is a moral obligation towards all his victims not to let this moment of catharsis be reduced to the formula: 'They got what was coming to them.' Instead, we must let it be a stimulus for the recognition of a similar evil seed among 'our own' people, because the mentality that fostered the phantasm of Greater Serbia is by no means exclusive to the Serbs. Greater Serbia can happen to anyone, in a whole range of forms that always begins lightly, festively, with an entertaining parade of political clowns and enthusiastic babblers in front of a sleepy audience which just shakes its head contemptuously at it all. But then it ends in a general bloody catastrophe in which even that sleepy audience is not spared.

The defeat of Milosevic's Serbia will be reduced by the extent to which anything of the mentality that created it remains among its neighbours; their future depends absolutely on the authenticity and consistency of that defeat. And, just as no one other than the Serbs can do their part of the work for them – recognition of the evil among them – they themselves cannot fundamentally defeat the idea of Greater Serbia that it would be possible to say that it had also been defeated as a syndrome among others.

The nebulous phrases associated for generations with 'Serbian Kosovo' hardly differ, for example, from the paratheological tirades of the then President of the Croatian Assembly, Nedeljko Mihanovic, at Bleiburg on 14 May 1995 [a small Austrian town associated with the train of refugees from communism heading for western Europe in 1945. The train was turned back to Yugoslavia by the Allies and all the refugees were massacred. In the numbers game – Croats killed more Serbs and vice versa – on the eve of the war in 1991, Bleiburg was repeatedly invoked as an example of yet another international, unacknowledged war crime – Tr]. With the help of shallow but suggestive Biblical comparisons and analogies, he too played the role of the prophet of a new religion of 'Croatdom', just as artificial and harnessed to daily political requirements, and just as devoid of the slightest trace of piety towards the dead, as that of the Serb mythmakers.

As Luka Vincetic wrote in these pages at the time, such a commemoration of Bleiburg 'was regretfully reminiscent of the final evocation of a "Croatian Kosovo"' and 'in this way, despite all our insistence that we did not belong to the Balkans, we were virtually following in the footsteps of the Serbs'. Here, too, there was a morbid reference to bones and 'Greater Serb sledge hammers', and the mythology of defeat, betrayal and revenge, national mystification and a pseudo-religious attitude to the nation, enduring weeping over the fate of the people and the accusation of the whole world, and it was clear to anyone who wanted to see that the laying of the foundation of the myth of 'heavenly Croatia' had already gained ground in just the same way as that of 'heavenly Serbia' had done.

This does not mean that such national mystification will develop to an analogous degree and have similar consequences. But Vincetic had good reason to warn people that this was precisely the way the idea of the Kosovo mythic fatherland had begun in Serbia. Today everyone in Croatia can see where Dobricca Cosic's pronouncements about 'eternal winners in war and losers in peace' have led Serbia, but it is worth recalling that, at a meeting of his party, one Croatian minister explained quite seriously that 'the Croats always won courageously in war, but always became the victims of the intrigue, cunning and diplomacy of their foreign enemies'.

The repetition of the idea of the Serbs as a 'heavenly people', which has in the end led them into misery and ruin, ought to be a cause for recollecting the recent message from the official military gazette about 'the millions of Croats in their heavenly homeland'.

Also, it is impossible not to feel horror at the words of a former Bosnian high functionary who found no better words to express the terrible sufferings of Srebrenica – probably unaware of the origin of his inspiration – than to call it 'the greatest underground Bosnian city'. That is precisely the morbid but so hypnotic catchphrase used of Jasenovac [WWII *ustachi* death camp in Croatia – Ed] – 'the greatest underground Serbian city' – dreamed up in the mid-80s by Matija Beckovic, one of the greatest Greater Serb 'murderers at a desk', whose hypnotic creations, in the hands of the demonic masters of propaganda, led directly to the fate of Srebrenica in the summer of 1995.

In the autumn of 1991, the Orthodox theologian Pavel Rak wrote an article in which he reacted to appeals for repentance which the leadership of the Serbian Orthodox Church was then sending in all directions. Not a day passed without some hypocritical bishop of humble and penitent expression, convinced of his own and his fellow-countrymen's God-given infallibility, listing all that the Serbs had suffered throughout their history. And there was not one neighbouring nation that was not accused of some crime committed by their members in the past. Rak offered such people for reflection a simple hypothetical situation:

> 'Let us just imagine what would happen if our enemies listened to the Serbian exhortations and all repented, fundamentally. Merciful God, who accepts the repentance of even the greatest sinners, would then forgive the enemies of the Serbs, while leaving us, who are convinced that everyone else ought to repent, just where we are, in a hell of hatred, because that is where we have shut ourselves.' ❑

Ivo Zanic *is an independent journalist in Croatia. This piece first appeared in the satirical weekly* Feral Tribune, *19 April 1999. Translated by Celia Hawkesworth*

KENDAL NEZAN

What's the difference between a Kurd and a Kosovar?

Turkey's Kurds ask why they have not benefited from the same international humanitarian concern as the Kosovo Albanians

After being pushed from pillar to post and hunted across Europe for four months, Abdullah Oçalan, leader of the Kurdish Workers Party (PKK), was finally captured in Kenya and handed over to the Turkish government on 15 February. His trial inside the island prison of Imrali prison began in May. This is the prison normally reserved for those already condemned to death and notorious as the place where the democratically elected prime minister, Adnan Menderes, and two of his ministers were executed in 1960. Oçalan has been leading an armed struggle against the army since 1984.

The Kurds feel humiliated and scorned, thrown back on an old adage born of long experience: 'The Kurds have no friends.' For many of them, Oçalan is the victim of a Turco-American-Israeli plot, brought to a successful conclusion with the complicity of the Kenyan and Greek governments. Hence the anger of the community and the spate of violent demonstrations against the embassies of these countries around Europe, the Middle East and the Caucasus following his capture. Under the guise of preventing further outbreaks, the Turkish authorities arrested 2,000 Kurdish and Turkish human rights activists in the space of one week, and banned the international media from Kurdistan.

Europe, which has frequently given refuge to corrupt Third World

Kurdish protestors hold painting of Oçalan. London, June 1999 – Credit: Judith Vidal Hall

dictators with blood on their hands, closed its doors to the Kurdish leader under pressure from Washington and for fear of Turkish economic reprisals, notably against its arms sales to that country. With their country on the verge of bankcrupcy and smarting from US criticism following the bomb attack on the US embassy in Nairobi in August 1998, the Kenyan leaders did what was asked of them in return for economic and political favours.

Athens' role in the affair is more puzzling. Public opinion, largely favourable to the Kurds, was shocked by this 'treachery' and Prime Minister Constantin Simitis was forced to sacrifice three of his ministers, including the minister of foreign affairs, Theodore Pangalos. The Greek

*Kurds protest against UK involvement in a dam project in Turkish Kurdistan,
London, June 1999 – Credit: Judith Vidal Hall*

authorities have still not explained why they transferred Oçalan to Kenya
on 2 February, but the country is well known as a staging post for Israeli
intelligence and for its vulnerability to US pressure. According to a
number of Turkish papers, Athens agreed to hand over Oçalan in return
for US and Turkish agreement to the installation in Crete of SS-300
missiles bought by Cyprus from Russia. However, there is probably a
good deal more to the story than this.

Since the fiasco of their secret intelligence operations in Iraq in 1996,
the USA has been in search of a new strategy to overthrow the Iraqi
regime. For this, the cooperation of Turkey, a NATO member, is
crucial, particularly the use of its Inçirlik airbase. To accommodate

Ankara, Washington put the PKK on the international terrorist list, even though the latter has never carried out any attack against US interests. But these things cut both ways: the ex-terrorist and once reviled Yasser Arafat is now a bosom pal of Bill Clinton

The PKK also presented a serious obstacle to another US project in the region: the implementation of the peace deal between the two main Iraqi Kurdish parties put in place by Madeleine Albright in September 1998. Both Syria and Iran were using the PKK to upset this *pax americana*. Given its plan to promote democracy in Turkey and secure its integration into the European Union, Washington saw the PKK and its leader as 'expendable', 'enemies to be defeated'.

Israel claims it had no direct part in the operation against Oçalan. However, it was its intelligence organisation, Mossad, that first informed Ankara of Oçalan's presence in Moscow in October 1998; Israeli advisers are also involved in the training of Turkish special forces fighting the PKK. On 4 February this year, the columnist William Safire alleged US-Israeli cooperation in the arrest of 'the evil Kurd, Oçalan' in the *New York Times*.

Unlike their Ottoman predecessors, who out of respect for their adversary confined themselves to deporting rebel Kurdish leaders, subsequent Turkish governments have hanged the leader of every Kurdish uprising this century. In conformity with a tradition established by Atatürk himself, Oçalan will be condemned to death for high treason under article 125 of the penal code and hanged following a show trial.

Several western governments as well as lawyers have called on Ankara to ensure that Oçalan is given a fair trial. In a country where the courts have handed down a 200-year prison sentence to the Turkish intellectual Ismaïl Besikci merely for his writings on the Kurds; and where appeals by Kurdish MPs for a fair trial did nothing to stop their condemnation to 15 years in prison for expressing their opinion, this is a vain hope.

On 5 September 1937, Seyit Riza, the leader of a Kurdish rebellion, was captured by Turkish troops. To celebrate the event, Atatürk decided to go in person to the region on 30 November, officially to open a bridge on the Euphrates. Learning that certain local notables were planning to 'appeal' to the 'father of the nation' to spare the life of the condemned man, Ihsan Sabri Caglayangil, who was to become President of the Republic in the late-1970s, records in his *Anilarim* (Memoirs): 'The government rushed me down to the region so that those who were to be hanged could have their sentence carried out before Atatürk arrived.'

Caglayangil arrived on Friday evening, 27 November, and went straight to the prosecutor, who explained that the court could not be convened on Saturday since this was a holiday. On the advice of the deputy prosecutor, an old friend from his days teaching in the university, he appealed to the governor – who sent the prosecutor 'on holiday'. He then went to the judge, who also argued that legally he could not convene the court before Monday, 30 November. However, in the event, the court was assembled during the night of Sunday/Monday in a room lit by hurricane lamps. Acting on instructions, it condemned the Kurdish leader and six of his associates to death.

No appeal was allowed; General Abdullah Pasha, the supreme military authority in the region, had signed the death warrant in advance on a piece of blank paper. At 3:00am, the condemned men were led to scaffolds lit by the headlights of police vehicles. The 75-year-old Kurdish chief mounted the scaffold and, brushing aside the hangman, put the rope around his own neck and with his last words promised: 'You have not seen the last of the Kurds; my people will avenge me!' Next day, Atatürk arrived for his visit. Justice had been done, the proper formalities had been observed and the Kurdish rebellion had been 'decisively put down'.

The PKK is under no illusions and has been encouraging its militants to give meaning to Oçalan's words: 'My death will serve the Kurdish cause better than my life.' On 18 February, a presidential council of the PKK that included Cemil Bayik, number two in the organisation, Osman Oçalan, brother of 'Apo', and Murat Karayalcin, read a communiqué on Med-TV calling for 'the extension of the war to all civilian and military targets in Turkey and Kurdistan' and for 'continuing peaceful demonstrations abroad' (see p27).

In effect, this new direction envisages that 'from now on, every member of the PKK will live and fight like *fedayin*', that 'Turkey is wrong to exult' and that 'before long [Turkey] will come to regret the removal of Oçalan, who did everything in his power to prevent the conflict between his organisation and the Turkish army from degenerating into a broader Turkish-Kurdish war'. The PKK press regularly publishes editorials calling for a radicalisation of the struggle arguing that since the world has been made impossible for the Kurds, they should make it a hell on earth for the Turks and their western allies.

It would be a mistake to brush off such threats; they are born of despair. But Turkey remains deaf to the most basic demands – the Kurd's right to use their own language, for instance. In a statement in the daily *Milliyet* on 19 February, President Suleyman Demirel rejected any opening and confirmed that there was no question of allowing the Kurds to have schools or media in their own langauge since this would inevitably lead to 'the partition of the country'. According to the leftist, ultra-nationalist prime minister Bulent Ecevit who was responsible for the invasion of Cyprus in 1974, the capture of Oçalan would settle 'once and for all' the 'so-called Kurdish question, a problem fabricated by foreign organisations'.

There are around 850,000 Kurds living in various western European countries and the constant exodus provoked by the war raises increasingly serious concerns about public order. It is, therefore, in the interest of western governments to intervene with Ankara. They alone have the power to force Turkey's hand in recognising the existence of its 15 million Kurds and finally according them an acceptable status. This is no different in its way from the efforts of the contact group to impose measures on Serbia to ensure the protection of 1.8 million Kosovo Albanians. The Kurds are weary of the West's double standards. Are they going to be the only people with such a large population to enter the 21st century without any legally acknowledged existence? ❑

Kendal Nezan is the president of the Kurdish Institute in Paris. First published in Le Monde Diplomatique *March 1999. Translated by Judith Vidal-Hall*

IRENA MARYNIAK

Sadly mythed

The future map of the Balkans is taking shape as a segregated patchwork of monoethnic regions and states, vying for territorial and political supremacy – and for the best story

There is a story in Ivo Andric's 1940s epic *The Bridge over the Drina*, about the abduction of a pair of newborn twins by the Turks and their burial – alive – in the foundations of a mediaeval bridge that joins Bosnia and Serbia. It is dreamed up as part of a Serb plot to undermine a Turkish building project, Andric tells us, and perpetuated into legend by a woman who goes out of her mind and believes it. But the history is secondary, it's the myth that sticks. Because that's what Christian children in villages, centuries on, know to be true.

In Serbia and Montenegro, tales about the 1389 battle of Kosovo, which brought 500 years of Ottoman domination to the region, have been recounted and sung ever since. Slavs who converted to Islam were viewed as traitors – they had privileges Christian Serbs didn't – and the mass murder of their descendants in 1991 was perceived by many people in Serbia as just retribution for centuries of victimisation and abuse.

Yet in Tito's Yugoslavia (that 'nice' country, the freest in eastern Europe) people of different religions and languages lived side by side, travelled abroad if they wanted and watched US films together. Tito himself was a Croat and his power-base depended on maintaining an ethnic balance that ensured the Serb majority couldn't dominate. In state documents, it was thought best to avoid the words 'minority' and 'majority'. Instead, the federal constitution of 1974 drew a distinction between *narodi* ('peoples' or 'nations') and *narodnosti* (usually translated as 'nationalities' and in one, aborted, version of the constitution as 'peopalities'). The 'peoples' were the Slavic founders of the Yugoslav state: Serbs, Croats, Slovenes, Montenegrins, Macedonians and Muslims.

Narodnosti were the rest, the lot who mostly had a country somewhere else: Albanians, Hungarians, Slovaks, Romanians, Italians or Romanies. When Croatia proposed the transformation of Yugoslavia into a confederation, in 1990, Serbia objected on the grounds that this would relegate Croatian Serbs to a 'peopality'. Peoples have an internationally acknowledged right to self-determination. 'Peopalities' don't.

Ever since, hounded 'peopalities' have been seeking shelter in territories with supportive mythologies where they hope to be recognised as people: Bosnian and Croatian Serbs in Serbia; Serbian Croats in Croatia; Vojvodina Hungarians in Hungary; Kosovo Albanians in Albania and Macedonia; Sandzak Muslims in Muslim-controlled parts of Bosnia; Kosovo Serbs in Serbia; and Roma wherever they can safely lay their heads.

In western parts of Macedonia, where most people are Albanian, Slavic Macedonians are selling up and relocating to the Macedonian-dominated east of the country. Tetovo, 30 miles east of Skopje is chock-full of Kosovar refugees who have moved in with relatives or host families, along with KLA members who have come in with them. Ominously, at the end of April, three people were injured when a bomb went off close to Skopje's biggest market which acts as an unofficial border between the Albanian and Macedonian suburbs of the city.

Novy Sad, the capital of Vojvodina, has of course seen many more bombs in recent weeks. Its inhabitants – Hungarians, Slovaks, Romanians, Croats and Ruthenians, as well as Serbs – have been terrorised not just by missiles and burning oil refineries but by the prospect of retaliation on the ground. Vojvodina is the most prosperous and fertile part of Serbia, and was once the most ethnically diverse. It is also a stronghold of political opposition with fully formulated proposals for autonomy. Up to 20 per cent of the province's population of two million are Hungarian and, as a group linked to a NATO country, they face rising hostility. People have reported being thrown out of bomb shelters and roughed up, catholic priests have been threatened, churches firebombed, shop windows smashed. Schools, farms and hospitals are closed to accommodate Serb soldiers. Stories about paramilitary 'snatches' are rife.

'Kati', a teacher from Vojvodina, now in Hungary, says that despite the tensions there is still a distinction in people's minds between their neighbours, regular Serb forces and paramilitary groups. 'They can pick you up anywhere, in a disco, on the street. If you don't go they'll kill you,' she says. Her mother was on a bus one morning when it was stopped by three men with guns who took off all the young men on board. The paramilitaries have not been operating in Vojvodina yet – their 'conscripts' have been taken down to Kosovo – but people know that once the bombs have stopped, the real reprisals could begin.

Since the end of March, several thousand non-Serbs are reported to have left. This despite frontiers that have been closed to men of military age (except those with 4,000–5,000 marks to spare) and a 'green border' that has been protected on the Yugoslav side so tightly it's almost impossible to cross. But then deputy prime minister Vojislav Seselj, head of the Serbian Radical Party, has already said that he'll give Hungarians one sandwich to leave the country and Slovaks two, because they've a bit further to travel.

The past five to six years have seen the arrival in Vojvodina of over 100,000 Serbs from Croatia, to replace the 40,000–50,000 Hungarians who had already gone rather than face conscription, discrimination and negligible job prospects. Many have been 'allocated' Hungarian homes, vacated by owners awaiting the departure of Milosevic before returning. In that time the Hungarian-language press lost much of its funding, schools were trimmed down and Hungarian books removed from libraries and archives.

The local Hungarian leadership has had little choice but to remain pragmatic and conciliatory. The Mayor of Subotica and president of the Federation of Vojvodina Hungarians, Jozsef Kasza, has distanced himself from edgy nationalists in Budapest keen now to cash in on the action, and seek independence or the return of Vojvodina to Hungary. As the bombs dropped, he also warned about the dangers of Hungary playing an 'active' part in the war and said that insensitive media reports could have dire consequences.

This cautious posture, in potentially still very perilous circumstances, has been paralleled in the way parties representing other minorities – Muslims from Sandzhak or Romanies, for instance – are handling their predicament.

Sandzhak is an isolated mountainous region north of Kosovo, straddling southern Serbia and northern Montenegro. In 1991, over half of its 420,000 inhabitants were Muslim. By the time the Dayton Agreement was signed about 50,000 Muslims had left. When Serb forces

launched their 'draining the sea' campaign to oust the KLA from
Kosovo, last year, people thought Sandzhak might be next in line, an
anxiety fuelled when five Kosovo refugees were killed in a Sandzhak
village in the Montenegrin municipality of Rozaje in mid-April.

Some estimates suggest that since then 15,000-20,000 Muslims may
have crossed through Montenegro and Republika Srpska to Sarajevo,
and the Muslim-controlled parts of Bosnia. This is in spite of apparent
attempts by the Yugoslav army to maintain reasonably good relations
with Sandzhak Muslims and the fact that there have been no attempts to
mobilise them. Refugee families are now occupying the houses of
Bosnian Serbs who fled the suburbs of Sarajevo in 1996. Single-family
accommodation reportedly lodges up to 40 people, relieved and grateful
to be 'among their own'. The party representing their interests at home,
the Muslim Sandzhak Coalition, has kept its head well down.

The Romany Congress Party, which represents the gypsies, has been
even more pliant. Roma have been conspicuous at anti-NATO rallies
and in the press, expressing support for the Belgrade regime. But despite
feverish protestations of loyalty from their leaders, 20,000 Roma have
had to flee Kosovo into Serbia and Montenegro since March. Their
stories range from claims that this was just migration from an area of
high unemployment, to reports of murder and abuse both by the KLA
and by the Serb police. They are now packed into overcrowded
settlements with other gypsy families, lying low and refusing to talk to
journalists and human rights activists. Few have the documents necessary
to move on, and neighbouring countries are unlikely to be sympathetic.
There have already been unconfirmed reports of Roma turned back
from Bulgaria.

Yet the treatment of Roma within Serbia until the crisis had been
comparatively tolerant. The incidence of reported racial murder of
gypsies in the country was lower than in the Czech Republic, for
example, though recently there have been reports of beatings of Muslim
(as opposed to Orthodox) gypsies in Vojvodina, as well as Kosovo. As a
'peopality' *par excellence* with no territory to make them people, and no
mention at all in the new federal constitution of the Republic of
Yugoslavia, the Roma could so conveniently be forgotten. In a battered,
collapsing Serbia, gypsies may be spared systematic ethnic abuse, but they
are certain to face further social marginalisation.

In the southern Serbian town of Leskovac, recent graffiti – that barometer of the public mood – read, 'NATO surrender! or we'll all die here.' For over two months, people have lived in fear of bombs, poisonous fumes, depleted uranium, occupation and torture by Albanians. They have been fed on a diet of propaganda in which the US, NATO and the KLA are identified as a single terrorist group, threatening occupation and genocide. They were told the country had been infiltrated by 'traitors and fifth columnists'. Independent journalists and human rights activists in Serbia privately express fears that hit lists for summary execution had already been drawn up by Milosevic and his security services. Perhaps they have.

In conformity with the shape of the myth, President Milo Djukanovic of Montenegro, who has opposed Belgrade since 1996, was also branded a traitor just as the Slav Muslims once betrayed their country in favour of a good life under the Turks, so the Montenegrin leadership has brokered an alliance with the evil empire of the West. Montenegro is effectively besieged by Yugoslav troops and there have been predictions of impending civil war fomented by Milosevic.

The certainty so many Serbs seem to feel of being victimised, martyred even, has been demonstrably verified. Thousands of deaths and injuries apart, half the people employed before NATO attacks began are no longer working or have lost their jobs; 42 per cent of the adult population have left home to move somewhere safer. Many places have no electricity. Supplies of water, bread and milk are depleted. There is likely to be a low yield from Vojvodina, the granary of Yugoslavia, this year, threatening the food supply in the Serbian market as a whole.

The experience may also have consolidated parts of the community, creating deep rifts between those who stayed and faced the bombs, and those who didn't. But after the settlement, tribal and religious allegiance still beckons. It will take a great deal to rebuild the country, and the region, into something more than a segregated patchwork of monoethnic regions and states, vying for territorial and political supremacy – and for the best story. ❏

Irena Maryniak

Support for

Index on Censorship and the *Writers and Scholars Educational Trust (WSET)* were founded to protect and promote freedom of expression. The work of maintaining and extending freedoms never stops. Freedom of expression is not self-perpetuating but has to be maintained by constant vigilance.

The work of *Index* and *WSET* is only made possible thanks to the generosity and support of our many friends and subscribers worldwide. We depend on donations to guarantee our independence; to fund research and to support projects which promote free expression.

The Trustees and Directors would like to thank the many individuals and organisations who support *Index on Censorship* and *Writers and Scholars Educational Trust*, including:

Anonymous
The Ajahma Charitable Trust
The Arts Council of England
The Bromley Trust
The John S Cohen Foundation
Danish International Development Agency (DANIDA)
Demokratifonden
The European Commission
The Ford Foundation
Fritt Ord Foundation
The Goldberg Family Trust
The Golsonscott Foundation

The JM Kaplan Fund
The Open Society Institute
The Onaway Trust
CA Rodewald Charitable Settlement
The Royal Ministry of Foreign Affairs, Norway
The Alan and Babette Sainsbury Charitable Fund
Scottish Media Group plc
Stephen Spender Memorial Fund
Tom Stoppard
Swedish International Development Co-operation Agency
United News and Media plc
UNESCO

If you would like more information about *Index on Censorship* or would like to support our work, please contact Hugo Grieve, Fundraising Manager, on (44) 171 278 2313 or e-mail hugo@indexoncensorship.org

GREGORY PALAST

Nanwalek rocks

Incorporation did what earthquake and oil pollution had failed to achieve: it broke the Chugach – until the women took over

Until four years ago, a heavily armed rock-and-roll band held lock-down control of the politics and treasury of Nanwalek, a Chugach village, on the far side of Alaska's Kenai Fjord glacier.

Rock came to the enclave at the bottom of Prince William Sound in the 1950s when Chief Vincent Kvasnikoff found an electric guitar washed up on the beach. By the next morning, he had mastered it sufficiently to play passable covers of Elvis tunes. Of all the lies the natives told me over the years, this seemed the most benign.

We sat in the chief's kitchen facing an elaborate Russian Orthodox altar. It was a golden day, late summer at the end of the salmon run, but the chief's 18-year-old nephew hung out in the bungalow watching Fred Astaire movies. Fishing was excellent, the chief assured me. He'd taken 12 seals this year. I didn't challenge the old man, legless in his wheel-chair. Everyone knew he'd lost the boat when the bank repossessed his fishing licence. Besides, the seals had been poisoned eight years earlier in 1989.

On Good Friday 1964, the snow-peaked mountains of Montague Island rose 26 feet in the air, then dropped back 12 feet, sending a tidal wave through the Sound. In the village of Chenega, Chugach seal hunter Nikolas Kompkoff ran his four daughters out of their stilt house and raced up an ice-covered slope. Just before the wall of water hit, he grabbed the two girls closest, one under each arm, ran ahead, then watched his other two daughters wash out into the sound.

Chenega disappeared. Not one of the homes, not even the sturdier church, remained. A third of the natives drowned. Over the next 20 years, Chenegans scattered across the sound, some to temporary huts in other villages, others to Anchorage. Every Holy Week, they sailed to the old village, laid crosses on the debris and Kompkoff would announce another plan to rebuild. As the prospect of a New Chenega receded into improbability, Nikolas became, by turns, an Orthodox priest, a notorious alcoholic and failed suicide. He was defrocked for the attempt.

In 1982, Nikolas convinced his nephew Larry Evanoff to spend his savings building a boat that could traverse the sound. The boat was not finished until the winter had set in. Nevertheless, he sailed to Evans Island with his wife and two children. They built a cabin and, for two years, without phone or short-wave radio, a hundred miles from any road, they lived off seal, bear and salmon while they cleared the land for New Chenega. Over the next seven years, 26 of Chenega's refugee families joined the Evanoffs and, with scrap wood from an abandoned herring saltery, built a tiny church with a blue roof for Nikolas Kompkoff, whom they still called 'Father'.

On 24 March 1989, they commemorated the 25th anniversary of the tidal wave. The same night, the *Exxon Valdez* oil tanker ran aground and killed the fish, smothered the clam beds and poisoned the seals.

In mid-century, the average life expectancy for Chugach natives was 38 years. They had next to nothing by way of cash and the state moved to take even that away. 'Limited entry' laws barred them from selling the catch from their traditional fishing grounds unless they purchased permits that few could afford. They did have tenuous ownership of wilderness, villages and campsites, however. In 1969, the largest oil deposit in the US was discovered in Alaska's north. The Chugach campsite on Valdez harbour was the only place on the entire coast that could support an oil terminal. The strip of land grew in value to hundreds of millions of dollars. In June of that year, Chief Vincent's father, Sarjius, representing Nanwalek, and 'Father' Nikolas, representing the non-existent Chenega, agreed to sell Valdez to BP and Humble Oil (later called 'Exxon') – for one dollar.

The Alaskan natives could not afford legal counsel, so they were grateful when Clifford Groh, head of Alaska's Republican Party and the most powerful attorney in Alaska, volunteered to represent them without charge against the oil companies. Some months after signing the sale of Valdez, Groh took on work representing his biggest client yet, 'Alyeska' – the BP-Exxon oil pipeline consortium.

Before he was done with the Chugach, Groh transformed them

utterly and for ever. Groh incorporated them. The tribe became Chugach Corporation; the villages Chenega Corporation and English Bay (Nanwalek) Corporation. The chiefs' powers were taken over by corporate presidents and CEOs; tribal councils by boards of directors. Once tribe members, the sound's natives became shareholders – at least for the few years until the stock was sold, bequeathed, dispersed. Today, only 11 of Chenega's 69 original 'shareholders' live on the island.

I first met the president of Chenega Corporation, Charles 'Chuck' Totemoff, soon after the spill when he missed our meeting to negotiate with Exxon. I found him wandering the village's pathway in soiled jeans, stoned and hung over, avoiding the corporate 'office', an old cabin near the fishing dock. Years later, I met him again at Chenega Corporation's glass and steel office tower in Anchorage. The stern, long-sober executive sat behind a mahogany desk and an unused laptop. A huge map of Chenega's property covered the wall, colour-coded for timber logging, real estate and resort development.

It took a month for the *Exxon Valdez* oil slick to reach Nanwalek. Still, Exxon had not provided even simple rubber barriers to protect the five lakes that spawned the salmon and fed the razor clams, sea lions, bidarki snails, seals – and the people of the ice. But when the oil did arrive, Exxon put virtually the entire populace of 270 on its payroll.

'The place went WILD. They gave us rags and buckets, US$16-something an hour to wipe off rocks, to BABYSIT OUR OWN CHILDREN.' In this roadless village that had survived with little cash or store-bought food, the chief's sister told me: 'They flew in frozen pizza, satellite dishes. Guys who were on sobriety started drinking all night, beating up their wives. I mean, all that money. Man, people went BERSERK.'

With the catch dead, the banks took the few boats they had and Chief Vincent's sister, Sally Kvasnikoff Ash, watched the village slide into an alcohol and drug-soaked lethargy. Sally said: 'I felt like my skin was peeling off.' Nanwalek's natives call themselves *Sugestoon*, Real People. 'After the oil, I thought: This is it. We're over. *Sugestoon*, we're gone unless something happens.'

Sally made something happen. In August 1995, the village women swept the all-male tribal council from office in an electoral coup plotted partly in the native tongue, which the men had forgotten. Sally would have become chief if Vincent, she says, hadn't stolen two votes. Once in power, the women returned native language to the school and replaced the rock-and-roll parties with performances of the traditional Seal and Killer Whale dances.

They put the village on a health-food regimen. 'We're fat,' says Sally, who blames the store-bought diet flown in twice-weekly from city supermarkets. The council banned alcohol. To show they meant business, the women jailed Sally's disabled Uncle Mack for bringing a six-pack into the village on his return from hospital.

The takeover set the stage for a battle with the real power, the corporation that, as owner of the land, collected millions annually from Korean logging companies. To protect its stockholders, the corporation resisted investments in hatcheries and other infrastructure which could restore fishing and shake the village out of its torpor. The corporation's president was a white man living in Anchorage. But unlike Chenega Corporation, the Nanwalek board included village natives, Chief Vincent's sons. They used their authority to maintain a monopoly on cigarette and junk food sales on Nanwalek. (Sally shut their lucrative operations.)

The chief's sons fronted a rock band, which had built a sound-wide reputation for dark, edgy music. They also had a reputation for violence or, at least, the threat of it. In one incident after the 'women's revolt', Bobby Kvasnikoff, the band's lead guitar, put an automatic rifle to the head of his cousin, Tommy Evans. Evans had avoided Nanwalek for years, but he'd accepted an invitation from the new council to return as health monitor. Bobby's armed greeting was meant to convince him that some family matters should remain secret.

But secrets are badly kept in Nanwalek. Evans' job was to staunch the spread of the HIV virus that had infected one in seven adults. It came with the oil, when Exxon's clean-up crews shared their needles and sexual appetites with village residents. Nanwalek's unhappy secret was the women's discovery that children had been molested by drunk, possibly infected, relatives.

I returned to Chenega in 1997 on the worst possible day. Larry, the pioneer of New Chenega, was out leading a crew cleaning up the tonnes of crude still oozing out of Sleepy Bay eight years after the spill. They'd lost a day's work that week for the funeral of Frankie Gursky, an 18-year-old who had shot himself after a drink-fuelled fight with his grandmother. Larry's team scoured the beach, his family's old fishing ground, but it wasn't theirs any more. The day before, the corporation had sold it, along with 90 per cent of Chenega's lands, to an Exxon-BP trust for US$23 million.

'Corporation can't sell it,' Larry said. 'People can't own land.' He rammed a hydraulic injector under the shingle and pumped in dispersants. 'The land was always here. We're just passing through. We make use of it, then we pass it on.' Nanwalek also sold. Before he died of AIDS, Bobby Kvasnikoff authorised Exxon's purchase of 50 per cent of the village land.

I was in president 'Chuck' Totemoff's office the day Exxon wired in the US$23 million for Chenega. When he moved out of the village, Totemoff announced: 'I hope I never see this place again.' Now he doesn't have to. I asked Chuck if, like some city-dwelling natives, he had relatives ship him traditional foods. 'Seal meat?' He grinned. 'Ever smell that shit? Give me a Big Mac any time.' ❏

Gregory Palast worked with the Chugach Native Alaska Corporation on its inquiry into allegations of wilful deception by oil companies, which led to the Exxon Valdez disaster in 1989. He writes a fortnightly column, 'Inside Corporate America,' for the Observer of London.

MARTIN CLOONAN

Bite pop

Britain's Broadcasting Standards Commission may not be a censor, but it is a watchdog with teeth – particularly when it comes to pop

Britain's Broadcasting Standards Commission (BSC), a 1997 amalgam of the earlier Broadcasting Standards Council and the Broadcasting Complaints Commission, is a strange beast. Established under UK statute law, it accepts complaints about unfairness and unsuitable content from viewers and listeners which it then investigates and asks broadcasters to explain. Its standards panel (a group of government appointees) will then review the complaint and come to one of three decisions: to uphold in part or in whole or to reject it. In the last case, the commission can require broadcasters to broadcast its finding but, other than this, has no power to impose fines or punish errant broadcasters.

From time to time, the BSC commissions research into various aspects of broadcasting such as the effect of swearing, sex and violence, or the impact of television on children.

The commission denies any censorial role but is is highly sensitive to accusations that it acts as such, claiming that it merely investigates complaints. However, broadcasters do not simply ignore the BSC; some may even tailor their programmes to avoid possible complaints, a not unreasonable form of self-censorship given that the number of complaints that are upheld is rising.

In its first bulletin since the merger (May 1997), the BSC reported 10 complaints upheld; the March 1999 bulletin contains 22. Does this reflect the increasingly 'objectionable' content of British broadcasting, or a more rigorous response from the BSC? Interestingly, the last two editions of the bulletin have seen a marked increase in instances of popular music falling foul of the Commission. More often than not, complaints occur when a track has been edited for radio – a process normally involving the removal of swear words – but the unedited version gets played by a DJ in prime-time listening.

In February this year, the bulletin listed two upheld complaints against unnamed pop records. The guilty radio stations were Silk FM and CD UK. In March, complaints against record content were upheld against Beacon FM and Radio 1. In the preceding year, there had been no successful complaints against pop music. The BSC also regularly upholds complaints against speech content of radio programmes, including those on Radio 1.

While it is too early to speak of a trend, it is clear that pop is figuring more in the BSC's bulletins than it has in the past. Whether this is due to pop becoming more offensive or listeners more vigilant remains open to speculation.

Two further points are worth making: the music industry routinely censors music it wants to get radio-play for. The pressing of tracks especially edited for radio-play, in addition to the original versions, is widespread. Should a DJ play an unedited version of the track, even in error, the BSC is increasingly likely to uphold a complaint against the station. ❏

Martin Cloonan is the author of Banned – Censorship of Popular Music in Britain: 1967-92 *(Arena 1996)*

JEROEN DE KLOET

Confusing Confucius

China's efforts to control 'dangerous music' are as illusory as the social harmony censorship is supposed to enforce

There were two dangerous kinds of music, said Confucius, loud and jarring and stimulating chaos, or 'pleasing but lewd'. Both disturbed the harmony he considered crucial for society. Were Confucius alive today, he would be pleased to hear that the authorities share his view. But on inspection of the contents of a Beijing music store, the philosopher could be forgiven for thinking things were not quite as they seem. Record companies, publishers and musicians employ a battery of subterfuges to circumvent censorship and fool its enforcers.

Rock is big in China but, since the government is afraid of large gatherings of young people, most rock performances are driven semi-underground. You find Beijing punks in the bar Scream and more established rock bands in Keep in Touch. Even when they subscribe to the police protection rackets, bars can still run into trouble. 'The police just come to make sure no one dances and that there is not too big an audience,' said former bar owner Fei Li. 'If you have 15 seats in the bar, you can only have 15 customers. Any more than that, you might run into trouble. But you can never tell; sometimes they allow, sometimes they don't.' The only thing anyone is sure of is that they can be sure of nothing.

Unlike other markets, where laws of supply and demand have taken over, the government remains a key player in the music industry. Only state-owned music publishers are licensed to release albums. Record companies contract the artists and record their music, but are dependent on the publishers to get their product into the market place. In the case of local albums, the publisher also has to make sure it is acceptable to the authorities. The state or the Party must not be criticised, and 'obscene' or 'pornographic' lyrics are banned. Song Ping, from one of China's

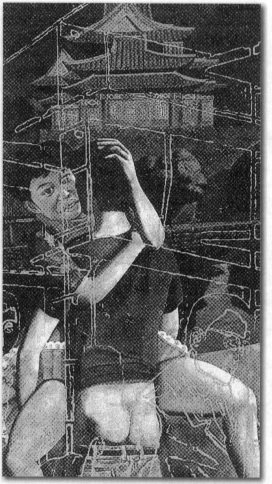

Sleeve artwork 'The Fly'

biggest music publishers, is clear what happens when an artist doesn't play by the rules: 'We just cut the inappropriate parts out.' Imported albums face fiercer scrutiny and are limited to an annual import quota of 300 titles a year. But producers and publishers, have joined forces to get controversial music into the market.

Anthony Chow, a manager with the Hong Kong-based record company Red Star says, 'We warn them to avoid any political content in their lyrics. They are pretty clever and usually write more about personal issues.' But sometimes the company deliberately sets out to fool the state-owned publisher. The lyrics of China's punk-rock classic 'Garbage Dump' by He Yong run: 'The world we are living in/is like a garbage dump/people are just like worms/fighting and grabbing/is there hope? is there hope?' Magic Stone's Wei Yan explains how they got approval: 'We were lucky. When we presented it to the publishing house we started playing a He Yong ballad and showed the MTV video of that song. They thought it wasn't bad and we quickly moved on to another album. In the end, they approved the album.'

In other cases, the publishers themselves are involved in the subterfuge. Jason Lee succeeded in releasing an album by Wang Lei: 'The publisher knew that some of the lyrics might lead to problems, but then they also knew how to play the game. They simply didn't send anything to the censorship department. So far there's no problem.'

The record company Jingwen faced problems with the release of the band Zi Yue. 'We changed one song, not because of political, but because of its sexual content,' said manager Wang Ming. 'Now we just play the waiting game; we simply drag our heels until they lose interest and we can release the album.' Zi Yue's fans had to wait a full year before the company finally released the album.

Zi Yue encodes its message in metaphors and images easily understood by its fans. Others play linguistic games, as in Wang Yong's album *Samsara*. 'We often coin words to replace the prohibited lyrics on the jackets which are similar in pronunciation,' says Magic Stone's Wei Yan 'For instance, Wang Yong's lyrics *'wo jiu qu ni made'* (I will fuck you) was changed to *'wo jiu qu ni ma?'* (shall I marry you soon?). The sung version keeps the 'dirty' words, but the lyrics on the jacket are sanitised. The same was done with a song from grunge band The Fly on a compilation tape: *'xing'* (sex) becomes *'xin'* (heart), and *'zuo ai'* (making love), *'cuo ai'* (loving wrongly) on the sleeve.

Sometimes the lyrics are simply not printed on the jacket at all, as was the case with 'Like a Knife' by the godfather of Chinese rock, Cui Jian. Controversial images on the jacket of *Zhou Ren*, such as a portrait of Chairman Mao, were pasted out on the mainland, though not in Hong Kong and Taiwan.

Despite the tricks and self-censorship, songs still get prohibited or are forced to conform to publishers' demands. The track '1966' on *Cobra*, which takes the Cultural Revolution as its theme, was banned outright; 'Traffic Accident' by Zi Yue faced the same fate. Once again, sex, not politics, was the culprit: 'My ass keeps on moving up and down/accompanying you into yet another orgasm/You boast of the unique odour on your body/suggesting I come/and laugh like you.' The Fly's debut album can only be bought underground: its lyrics, and the jacket depicting a naked and copulating couple, would never have got past the censors.

Censorship is a cat-and-mouse game. When the play has gone on for over 10 years it gets frustrating. 'The government plays a child's game that I cannot play,' says Cui Jian. 'You can treat them as kids or maybe you should just lie, or be patient. It's the only way to win.' ❏

Jeroen de Kloet *is working on Chinese popular music at the Amsterdam School of Social Science Research*

MARAT GUELMAN

Smashing time

At Moscow's *Art Manège* fair last December, Avdei Ter-Oganian, director of the School of Contemporary Art in Moscow, mounted a performance encapsulating his view that the contemporary art world in Russia has sold out to the money and taste of the *nouveaux riches*.

Posing as a provincial artist responding to foreign cultural influences by aping western radicalism, Ter-Oganian offered to 'sell' modish 'degeneracy' to any paying customer. The 'young nihilist' could desecrate a mass-produced religious icon for 50 roubles; the 'client' could desecrate an icon under the tutelage of the 'nihilist' for 20 roubles; 'desecration consultations' could take place at the client's home for 10 roubles.

Fair-goers entered into the spirit, laying into the icons with a hatchet; one was painted over with a profanity. Even though these were no more than commercial lampoons of the real thing, there were objections and Ter-Oganian's exhibit was closed.

The controversy intensified when Orthodox priests appeared on TV and in the press proclaiming that art in general must be controlled because 'the artist's soul is the easiest target for Satanic temptation'.

State officials made common cause with religious zealots – 'Orthodoxy is the basis of Russia's political and judicial system' and Ter-Oganian and his supporters are 'enemies of the state' – and the Moscow prosecutor charged the artist with 'incitement to religious hatred'. He is awaiting trial. ❏

Marat Guelman is the owner of the Guelman Gallery in Moscow. Information about Ter-Oganian's case is available in Russian at www.guelman.ru.

JIM D'ENTREMONT

Preachers of doom

Moral panic in the wake of the Columbine High School shootings produced an unprecedented wave of censorship initiatives from politicians and activists on the left as well as the right – but nobody wants to ban the guns

On 20 April at Columbine High School in the Denver suburb of Littleton, 18-year-old Eric Harris and 17-year-old Dylan Klebold fatally shot 12 fellow students and a teacher, wounded 23 others, then killed themselves. In addition to two shotguns, a hunting rifle and a semi-automatic pistol, the pair had brought an array of bombs in an effort to produce as many casualties as possible.

The incident, the latest and worst in a series of similar events in US schools, precipitated the most insidious moral panic in recent history. Its aftershocks rumbled through Congress, the legislatures of all 50 states, every local government and school administration from Maine to Hawaii, the corporate boardrooms of the communications and entertainment industries and every classroom in the land.

Public reaction was heightened by the instant media frenzy. Broadcast news reports were lurid, shrill and charged with the assumption that once again pop culture had transmuted hapless teenage boys into criminals. Before the victims' bodies had been removed from the crime scene, TV stations were illustrating facile analyses of violence in America with clips from films like *Natural Born Killers* (ironically a satire on the media's love affair with crime), footage of Marilyn Manson concerts and snippets of video games.

Harris and Klebold were members of a small, loosely knit, vaguely goth-influenced group of social outcasts on the margins of a student population of 1,965. Because they wore black, western-style dusters, they were dubbed the 'trenchcoat mafia' by their conservative classmates. Early reports portrayed the youths as members of the self-proclaimed

Trenchcoat Mafia, an organised gang of death-rock fans who studied the
manufacture of bombs on the Internet when they weren't watching
porno-violent videos or playing depraved, addictive video games.

Early uncorroborated reports identified Harris and Klebold as
admirers of the much-demonised rock performer Marilyn Manson.
Soon after the shootings, 10 US Senators led by Kansas Republican Sam
Brownback, a long-time anti-rock crusader, demanded that
Seagrams/MCA, the parent company of Manson's record label, stop
supporting 'music that glorifies violence'. Crumbling under a barrage of
threats and invective, Manson cancelled a performance at Denver arena,
then abandoned his 1999 tour.

Reliable sources suggest that the murderers were not, in fact, Manson
fans at all, preferring the German industrial band Rammstein and the
recently disbanded ensemble KMFDM (Kein Mehrheit für die Mitleid –
No Pity for the Majority). Amid allegations that Harris and Klebold
were neo-Nazis (the massacre took place on Hitler's birthday), both
bands were soon misidentified as Nazi skinhead hate groups. When it
was revealed that lyrics of KMFDM's 'Son of a Gun' ('son of a gun,
master of fate/Bows to no god, kingdom or state') were displayed on
Eric Harris's website, stores began pulling KMFDM albums off their
shelves.

In addition to music, the righteous and the opportunistic targeted the
Internet, television, films, videos, video games, books, styles of dress,
and T-shirts. An unprecedented wave of censorship initiatives came from
politicians and activists on both right and left. Liberal Democratic
Congressman Edward Markey of Massachusetts joined forces with
conservatives, including presidential candidate Senator John McCain of
Arizona, to urge the White House to order a summit conference on
youth and media violence. Congressional leaders called for a new
investigation into pop culture by the Surgeon General of the United
States.

Alleging that Harris and Klebold were homosexual, hard-right
'family values' groups interpreted the Littleton shootings as proof that
gay expression must be curbed. Noting that the perpetrators had indeed
been singled out for anti-gay harassment by some of their victims, leftists
called for hate-crimes legislation, more stringent speech codes in
educational institutions and legally mandated standards of civility. Noting
that the perpetrators affected unconventional styles of dress, conservatives

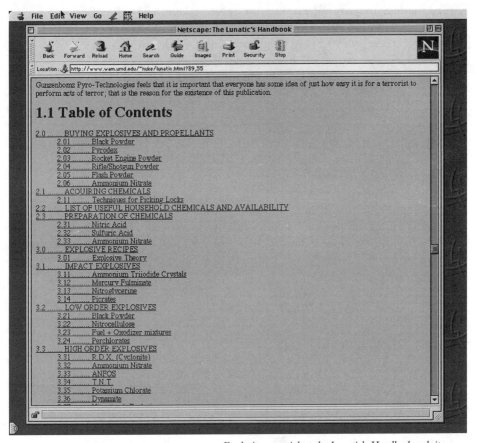

Explosive material at the Lunatic's Handbook website

called for increased regimentation, stricter dress codes, school uniforms, and bans on hair dye, unusual hairstyles, piercings, and 'occult' jewellery.

Across the nation there was a wave of disciplinary actions directed at students who wore trenchcoats or T-shirts promoting bands like White Zombie. In Hudson, Ohio, a nine-year-old boy was suspended from classes for writing a 'threatening' fortune cookie message ('You will die with honour') in response to an assignment. In Virginia Beach, Virginia, 16-year-old Chris Bullock was arrested when it was revealed that, in a

statewide Standards of Learning test he had taken in March – more than
a month before Columbine – he had answered a question with a fantasy
about a student threatening his school with a nuclear bomb.

Erupting at a time when individuals were announcing their
candidacies for the 2000 US presidential race, the Littleton tragedy was
swiftly exploited by candidates for public office. Decrying a culture that
'glorifies death', right-wing ideologue Gary Bauer formally declared his
presidential intentions one day after the shootings. Former vice president
Dan Quayle made the erosion of 'values' by popular culture the theme
of his campaign. Republican Senator McCain, who chairs the Senate
Commerce Committee, used the occasion to press for legislation
mandating Internet filtering software. Texas governor George Bush Jr,
the Republican frontrunner and a long-time opponent of gun control,
eagerly endorsed the 'media violence' interpretation of Littleton. Vice
President Albert Gore, Clinton's heir apparent, and his wife Tipper, co-
founder of the Parents Music Resource Centre, became ubiquitous
moralising presences.

The video games *Doom* and *Doom II*, which Harris and Klebold often
played, were cited as evidence that video games cause catastrophic anti-
social behaviour that must be prevented through strict regulation. FBI
agents investigating the backgrounds of Harris and Klebold searched
their video rental records for evidence of a connection between the
shootings and *The Basketball Diaries*, the 1995 film version of a memoir
by rock poet Jim Carroll. In the film (but not the book), a dream
sequence depicts a trenchcoat-clad Leonardo DiCaprio gunning down
fellow high school students. Because this sequence is alleged to have
inspired the 1998 murders of three students in Paducah, Kentucky,
parents of the victims have included Time Warner – whose subsidiary
Island Pictures produced the film – in a US$130-million lawsuit. A
similar suit is expected from the Littleton survivors.

Since 1992, 248 young people and adults have met violent deaths on
the premises of schools that serve 53 million students across the US. Six
mass shootings in schools have taken place in the past 18 months. On 10
May – less than three weeks after Littleton – six were wounded in a
'copycat' incident in Conyers, Georgia. In every school shooting
incident, a book, film, game, record or internet site – material ranging
from Stephen King's novel *Rage* to the music of rapper Tupac Shakur –
has been effectively scapegoated.

192   INDEX ON CENSORSHIP 4 1999

Though the availability of guns has now become a heated topic of debate, the National Rifle Association lost little ground in seeking to maintain the status quo. After Littleton, sweeping – though often cosmetic – gun-control legislation was introduced in Washington DC and in a number of states, and began to pass with reluctant support from Republicans. After 16 students and one adult were killed at Dunblane, Scotland in 1996, parliament banned private possession of handguns in the UK; in post-Littleton America, the legislation that becomes law may make it more difficult for the young, the unstable, or the criminally inclined to obtain firearms – but the US will continue to be armed to the teeth.

Legislative initiatives against popular culture, however, are likely to be more successful but may have broad, lasting and damaging effects. Violence in schools is one of the few surefire pretexts for censorship available to those who would suppress material they find ideologically offensive. Recent Congressional hearings – blatantly biased and stacked against freedom of speech – have promoted a constellation of repressive bills such as the Children's Protection from Violent Programming Act, which would prohibit 'violent video programming' from being broadcast when children are likely to be in the audience. Typical witnesses brought before Congressional committees have included Lt. Col. David Grossman, a military psychologist who insists that video games create killers, and morality *maven* William Bennett.

A minority of witnesses, like media analyst Robert Corn-Revere, have managed to point out that the proposed restrictions raise profound constitutional questions. A few, such as Professor Henry Jenkins of MIT, author of *From Barbie to Mortal Kombat: Gender and Computer Games*, have offered some thoughtful analysis. 'We don't want to deal with the fact that there's a specific political and social agenda behind these events,' says Jenkins, who notes that, among the materials alleged to be fomenting violence, are films and books that provide some of the most meaningful critiques of US violence available.

Efforts to understand and face up to the realities of US life have been almost absent from public debate in the wake of Littleton. The lives of Harris and Klebold received less consideration than the video games they played. Minimal attention was directed to the crushing conformity of superficially 'diverse' US culture, the quality of US education, the purportedly classless nation's preoccupation with status and the institutionally legitimised violence of the state.

In March, when NATO forces began bombing Yugoslavia, Eric Harris had been delighted. The son of a retired air force pilot, Harris unsuccessfully tried to join the Marine Corps five days before he opened fire on his classmates. On 21 April, the day after Harris's death at Columbine High, as US-led bombing progressed in the Balkans, President Clinton asserted that parents must teach their children to resolve disputes through 'words, not weapons'. On the day after NATO bombs killed 87 innocent refugees in Kosovo, Clinton was attempting to shame Hollywood producers into making less violent films.❏

Jim D'Entremont is head of the Boston Coalition for Freedom of Expression